ANY EASY INTIMACY

JEFFREY BROWN

D0009579

PUBLISHED BY TOP SHELF PRODUCTIONS
PO BOX 1282 MARIETTA GA 30061-1282

ISBN 189 183 0716
ISBN-13 978189 183 0716

2ND PRINTING. JUNE 2007
PRINTED IN CANADA

Carlos' Restaurant
429 Temple Avenue

1 Carlos

Tbl 70/2   Chk 727   Gst 2
                 Apr10'02 10:26PM

---

1 Cider	3.50
1 Coffee/Tea	2.75
1 Latte	3.50
1 Muscovy Duck	36.50
1 Vegetable Plate	32.00
2 Soup/Consome	15.00
2 Mixed Greens	13.00
2 Sorbet	8.00
2 Regular Dessert	19.00

FOOD	133.25
Tax	9.33
10:43 TOTAL	**142.58**

THANK YOU!
VISIT OUR WEB SITE
c̶_____.com
OPEN FOR LUNCH ON EASTER SUNDAY
MAKE YOUR RESERVATIONS EARLY
GIFT CERTIFICATES, PRIVATE ROOMS
   AND COOKING CLASSES AVAILABLE
   LOOKING FOR THAT SPECIAL GIFT

WE THINK YOU'D HAVE A LOT OF FUN TOGETHER

HEY, MARI AND I HAVE SOMEONE FOR YOU TO MEET
WHO?

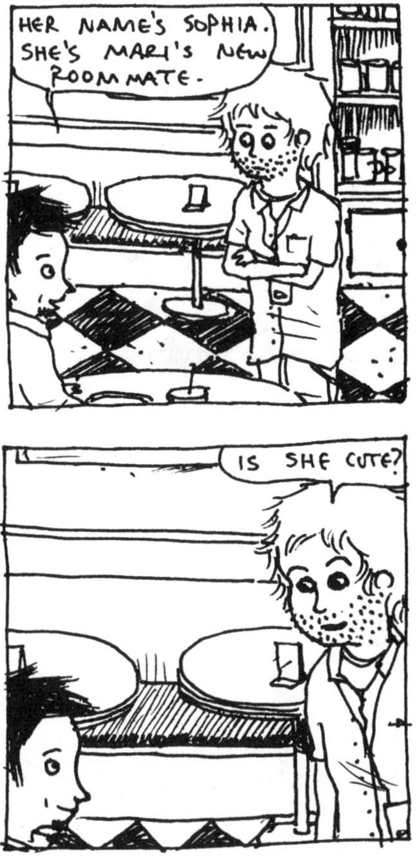
HER NAME'S SOPHIA. SHE'S MARI'S NEW ROOMMATE.
IS SHE CUTE?

BUT DOES SHE LIKE ME - LIKE ME

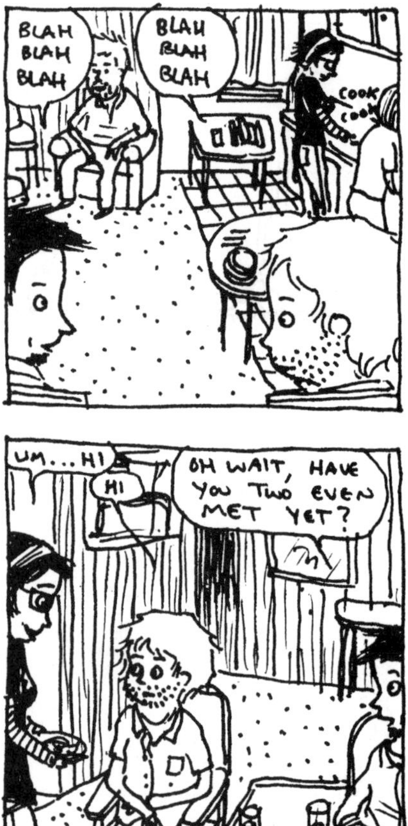
BLAH BLAH BLAH
BLAH BLAH BLAH
COOK COOK
UM...HI
HI
OH WAIT, HAVE YOU TWO EVEN MET YET?

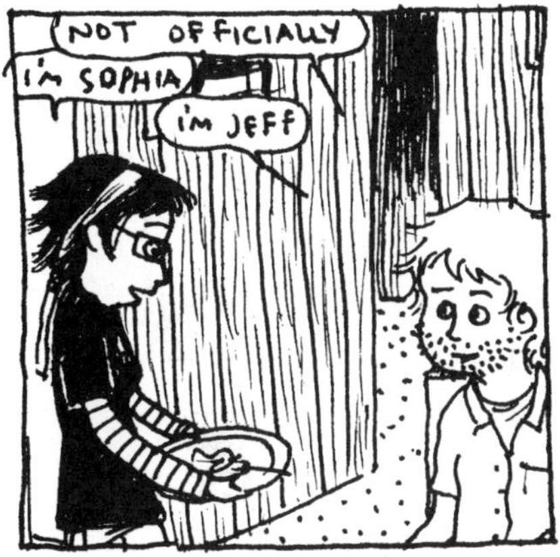
NOT OFFICIALLY
I'M SOPHIA
I'M JEFF

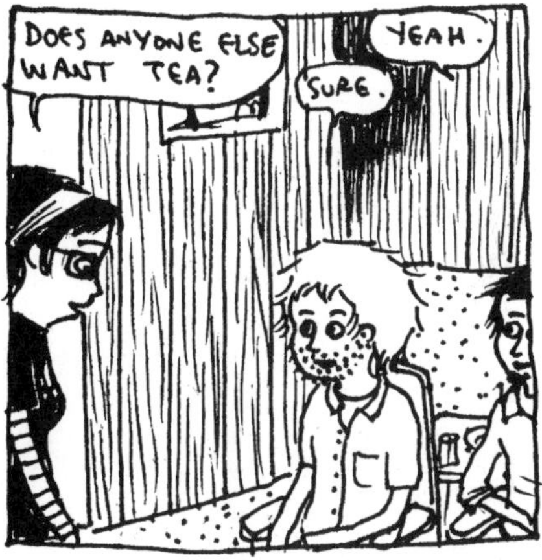
DOES ANYONE ELSE WANT TEA?
YEAH.
SURE.

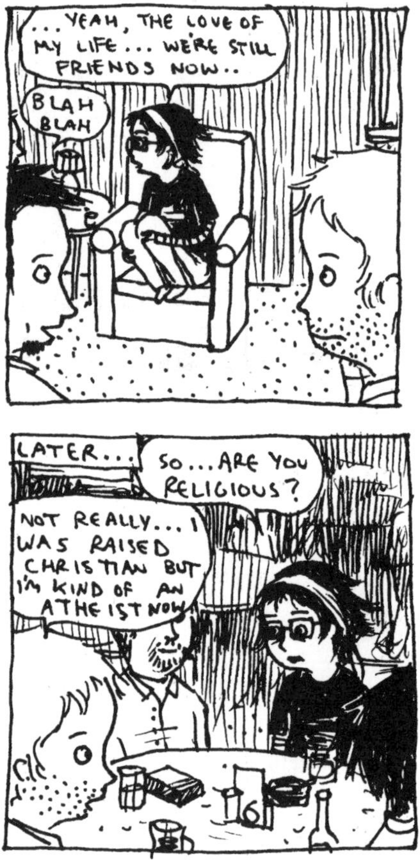
...YEAH, THE LOVE OF MY LIFE... WE'RE STILL FRIENDS NOW..
BLAH BLAH
LATER...
SO...ARE YOU RELIGIOUS?
NOT REALLY... I WAS RAISED CHRISTIAN BUT I'M KIND OF AN ATHEIST NOW

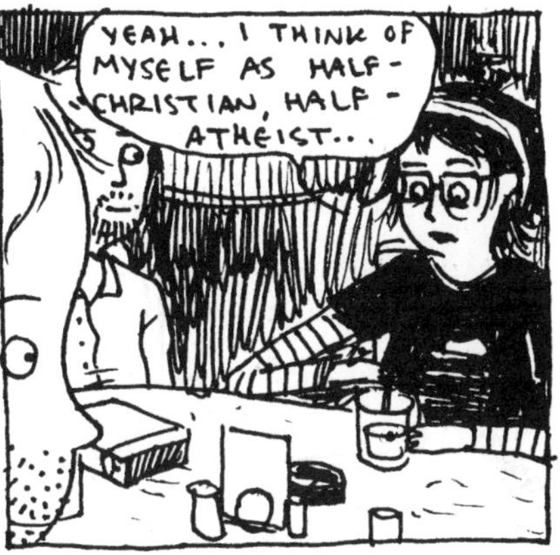
YEAH... I THINK OF MYSELF AS HALF-CHRISTIAN, HALF-ATHEIST...

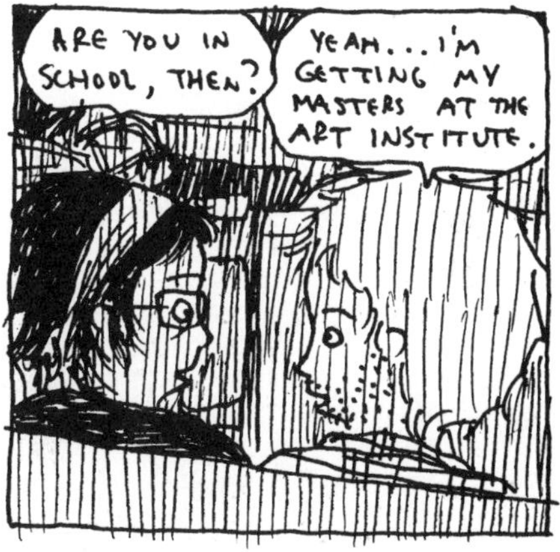
ARE YOU IN SCHOOL, THEN?
YEAH... I'M GETTING MY MASTERS AT THE ART INSTITUTE.

THE ROYAL TENENBAUMS

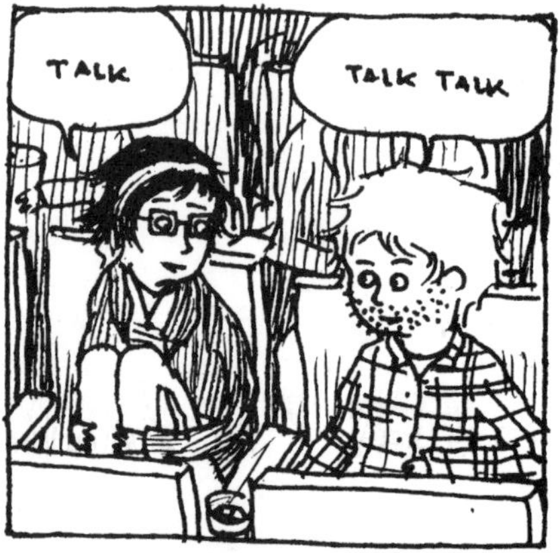
TALK
TALK TALK

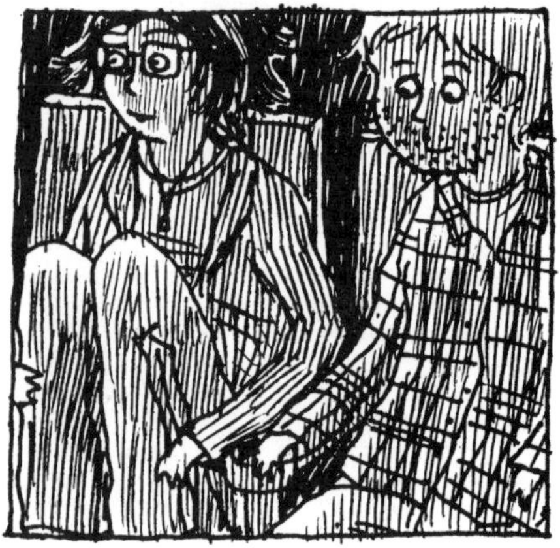

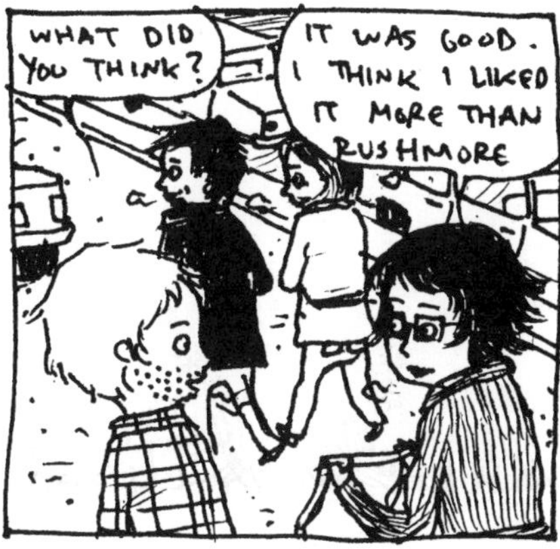
WHAT DID YOU THINK?
IT WAS GOOD. I THINK I LIKED IT MORE THAN RUSHMORE

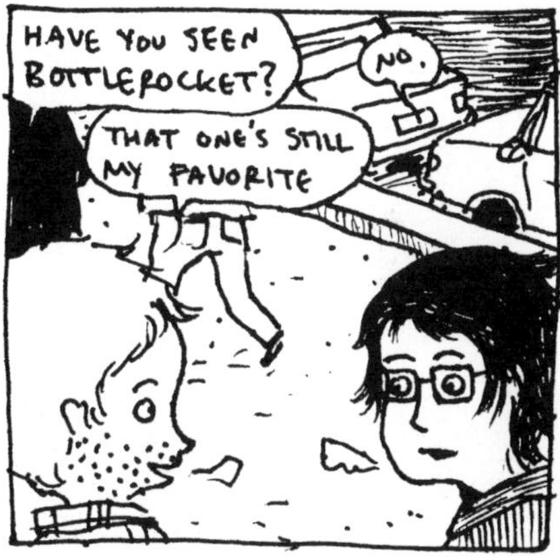
HAVE YOU SEEN BOTTLEROCKET?
NO.
THAT ONE'S STILL MY FAVORITE

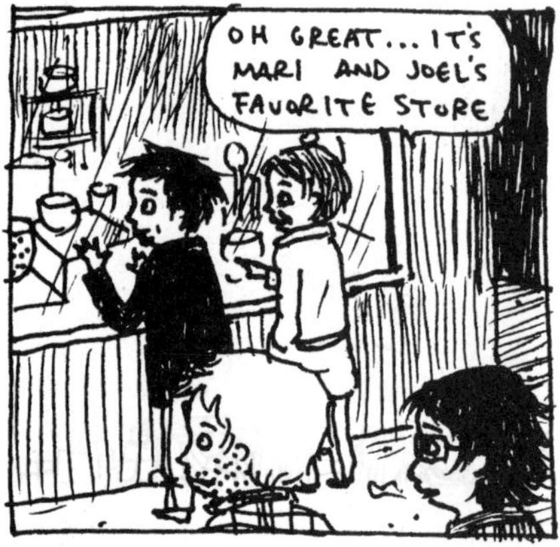
OH GREAT... IT'S MARI AND JOEL'S FAVORITE STORE

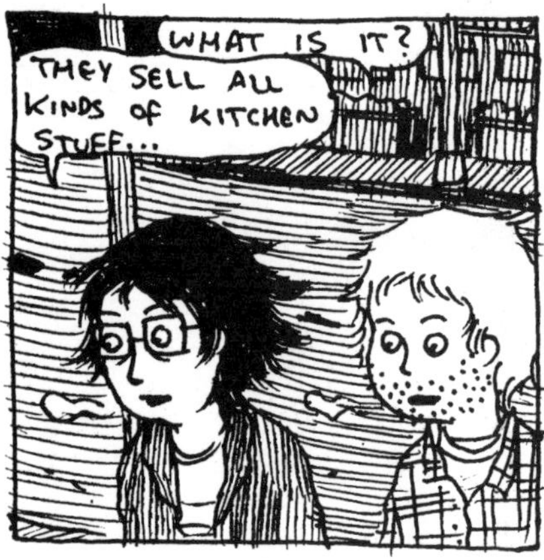
WHAT IS IT?
THEY SELL ALL KINDS OF KITCHEN STUFF...

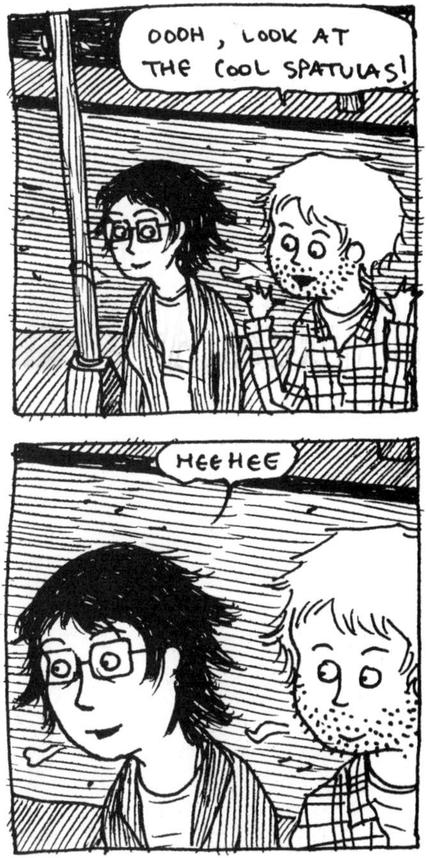
OOOH, LOOK AT THE COOL SPATULAS!
HEE HEE

YOU WORK TOMORROW? I CAN GIVE YOU A RIDE, SINCE I HAVE TO GO TO SCHOOL ANYWAY...
OH... OKAY
GOOD... THEN I DON'T HAVE TO GET UP...

HI.
HI.

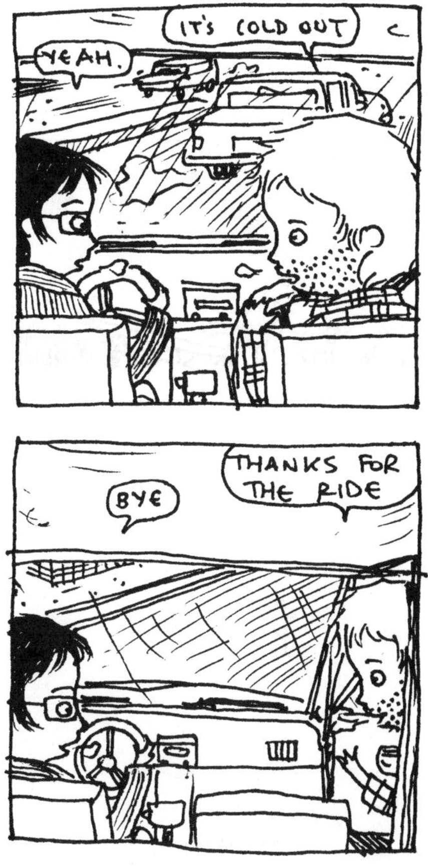
IT'S COLD OUT
YEAH.
THANKS FOR THE RIDE
BYE

JANUARY

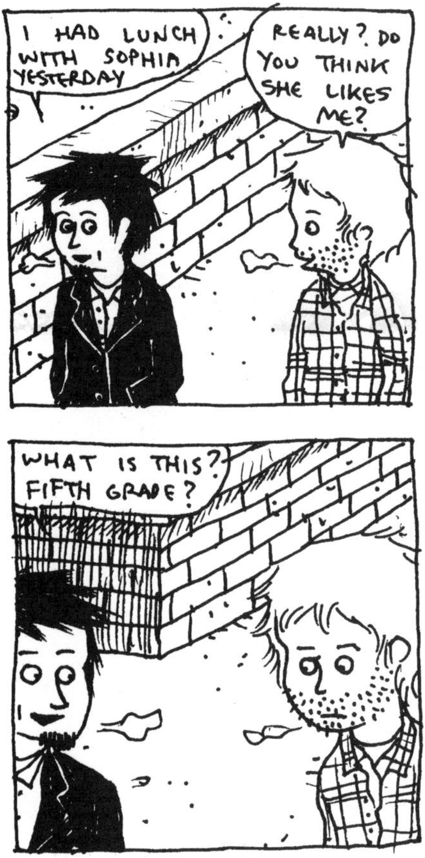
I HAD LUNCH WITH SOPHIA YESTERDAY
REALLY? DO YOU THINK SHE LIKES ME?
WHAT IS THIS? FIFTH GRADE?

ACTUALLY, SHE DID TALK ABOUT YOU. SHE THOUGHT IT WAS COOL YOU WERE IN GRAD SCHOOL...

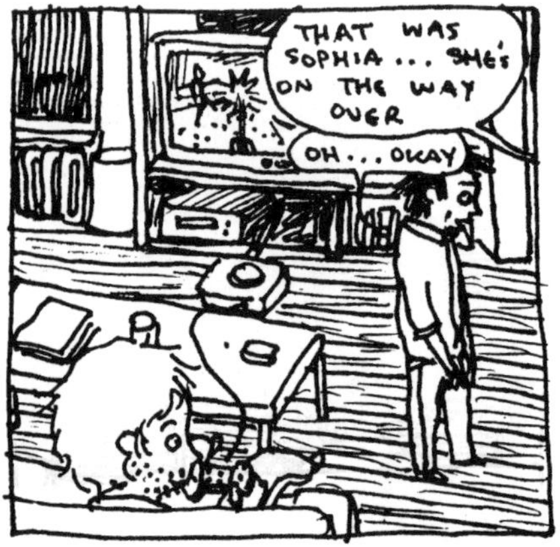
THAT WAS SOPHIA ... SHE'S ON THE WAY OVER
OH ... OKAY

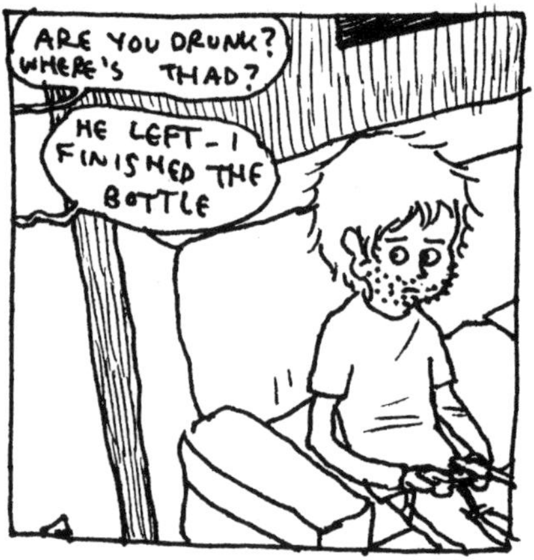
ARE YOU DRUNK? WHERE'S THAD?
HE LEFT - I FINISHED THE BOTTLE

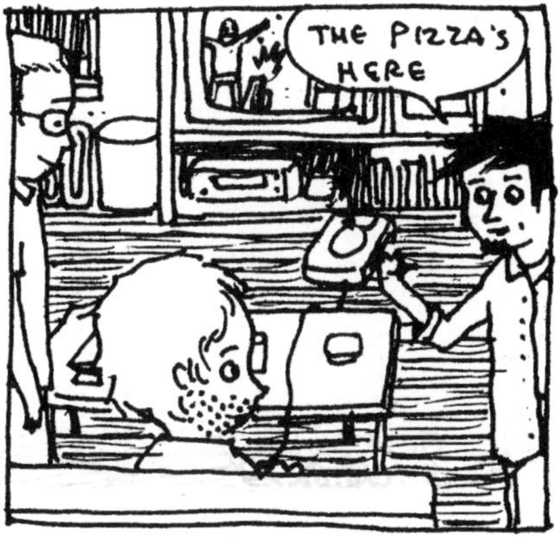
THE PIZZA'S HERE

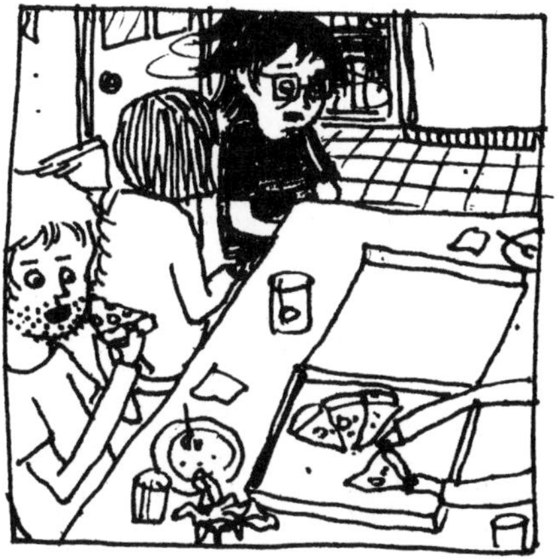

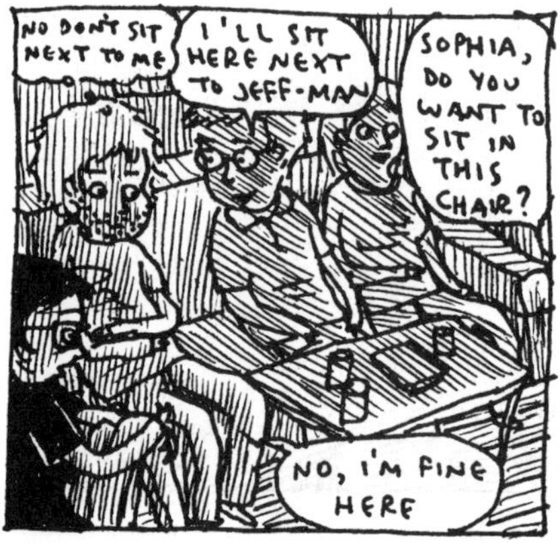
NO DON'T SIT NEXT TO ME
I'LL SIT HERE NEXT TO JEFF-MAN
SOPHIA, DO YOU WANT TO SIT IN THIS CHAIR?
NO, I'M FINE HERE

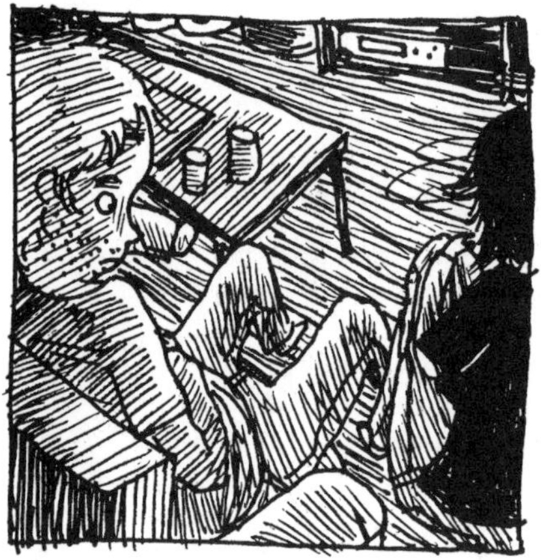

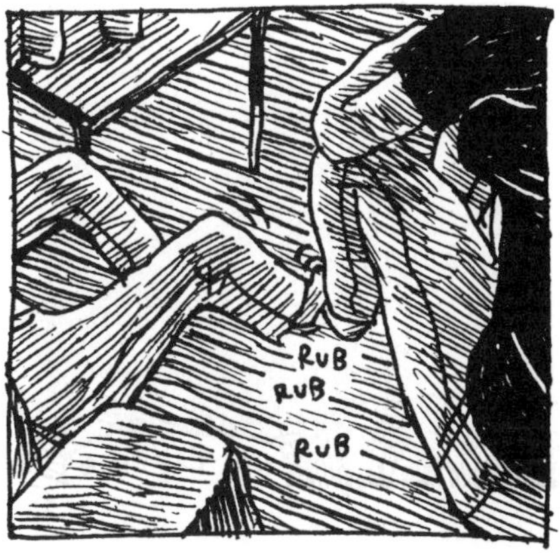
RUB
RUB
RUB

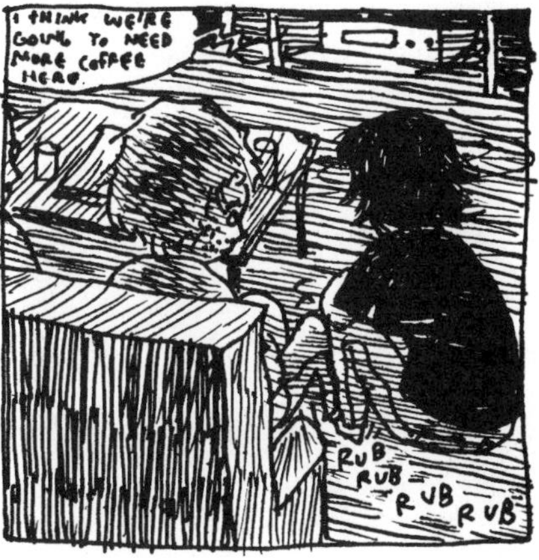
I THINK WE'RE GOING TO NEED MORE COFFEE HERE.
RUB
RUB
RUB
RUB

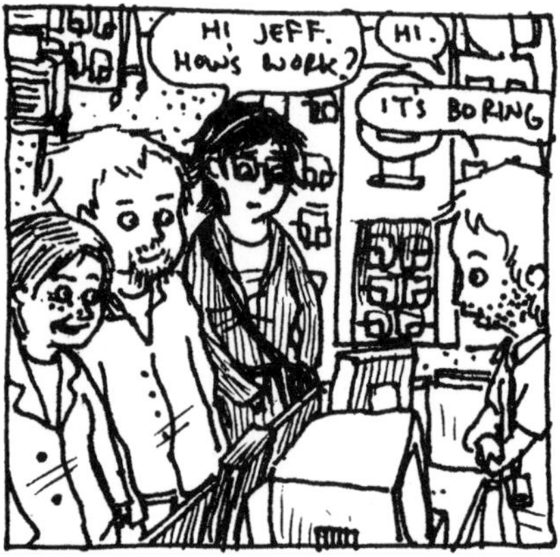
HI JEFF. HOW'S WORK?
HI.
IT'S BORING

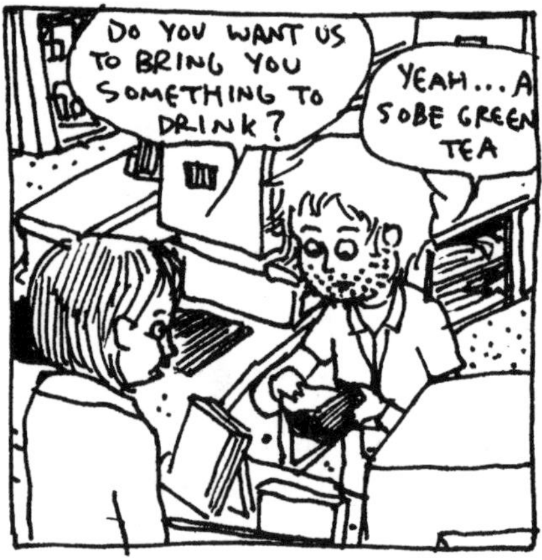
DO YOU WANT US TO BRING YOU SOMETHING TO DRINK?
YEAH... A SOBE GREEN TEA

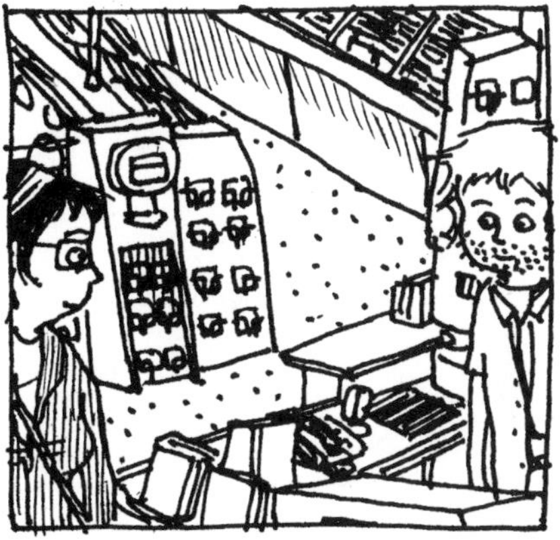

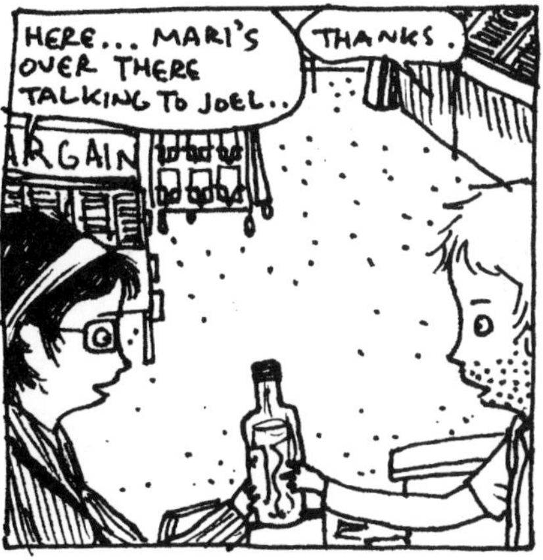
HERE... MARI'S OVER THERE TALKING TO JOEL..
THANKS.
ARGAIN

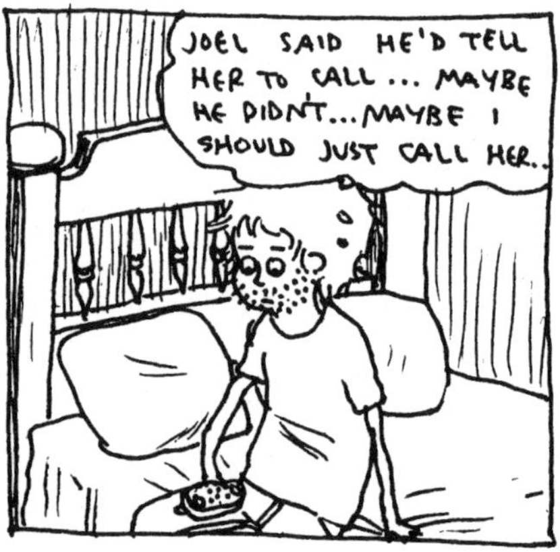
JOEL SAID HE'D TELL HER TO CALL... MAYBE HE DIDN'T... MAYBE I SHOULD JUST CALL HER..

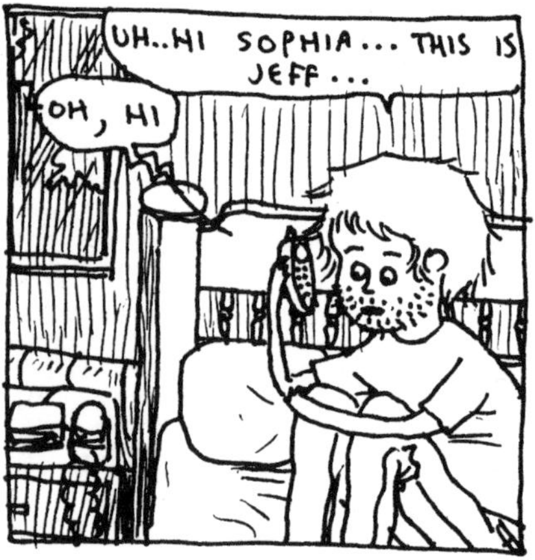
UH..HI SOPHIA... THIS IS JEFF...
OH, HI

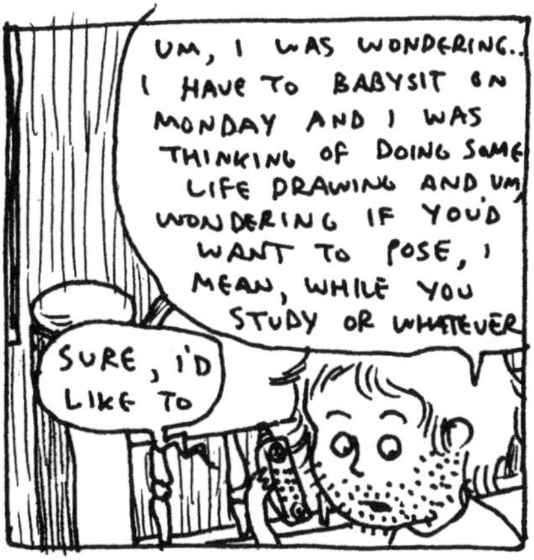
UM, I WAS WONDERING.. I HAVE TO BABYSIT ON MONDAY AND I WAS THINKING OF DOING SOME LIFE DRAWING AND UM, WONDERING IF YOU'D WANT TO POSE, I MEAN, WHILE YOU STUDY OR WHATEVER
SURE, I'D LIKE TO

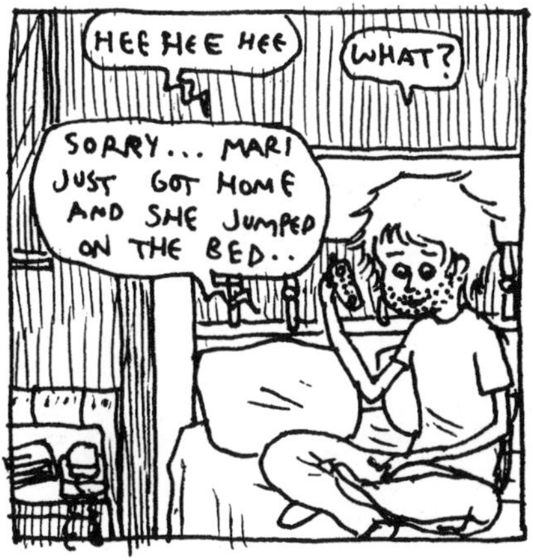
HEE HEE HEE
WHAT?
SORRY... MARI JUST GOT HOME AND SHE JUMPED ON THE BED..

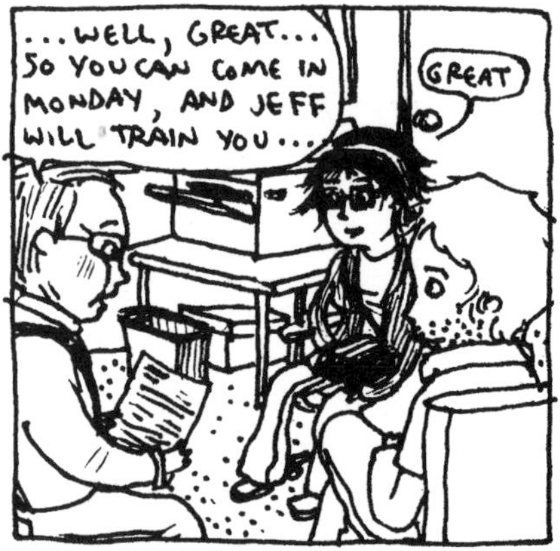
...WELL, GREAT...
SO YOU CAN COME IN
MONDAY, AND JEFF
WILL TRAIN YOU...
GREAT

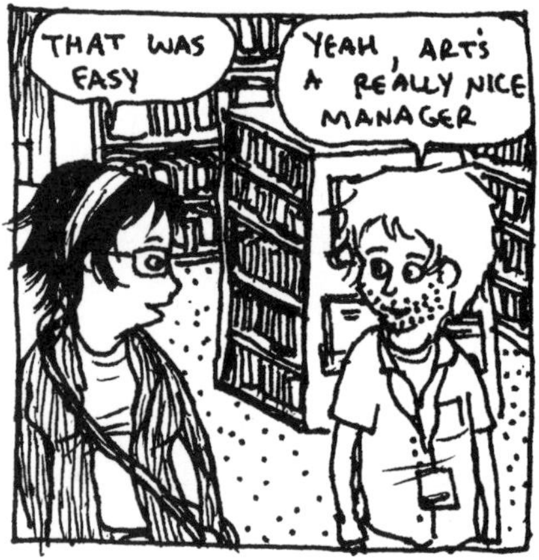
THAT WAS
EASY
YEAH, ART'S
A REALLY NICE
MANAGER

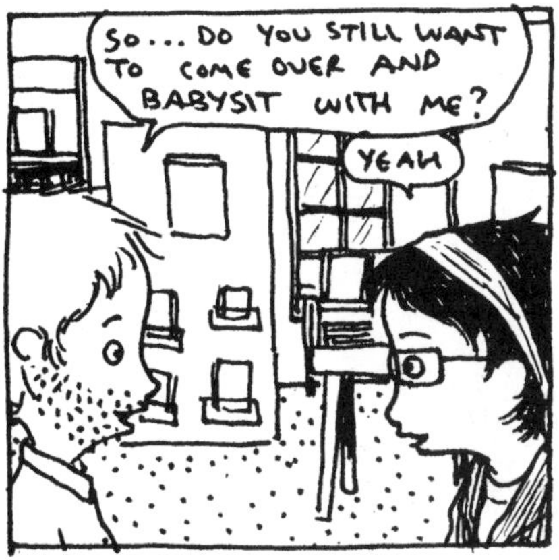
SO... DO YOU STILL WANT TO COME OVER AND BABYSIT WITH ME?
YEAH

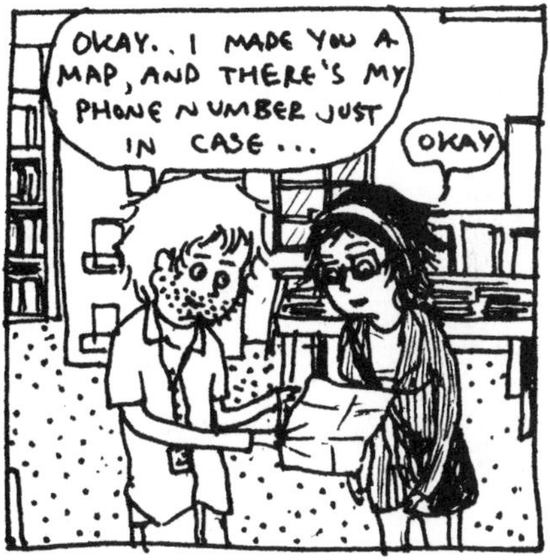
OKAY.. I MADE YOU A MAP, AND THERE'S MY PHONE NUMBER JUST IN CASE...
OKAY

THE LONG PAUSE BEFORE A FIRST KISS

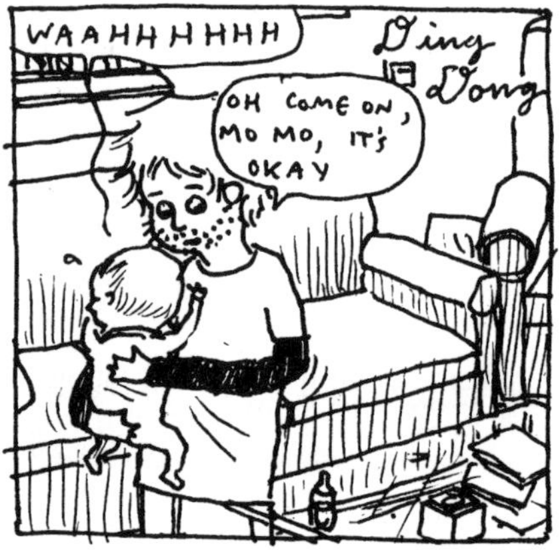
WAAHHHHHH
Ding Dong
OH COME ON, MO MO, IT'S OKAY

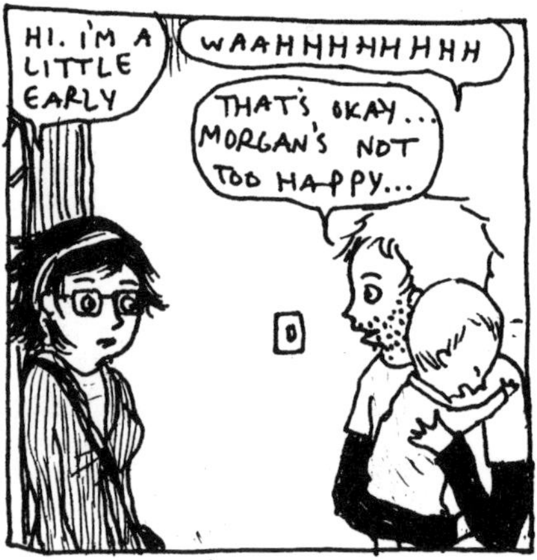
HI. I'M A LITTLE EARLY
WAAHHHHHHHH
THAT'S OKAY... MORGAN'S NOT TOO HAPPY...

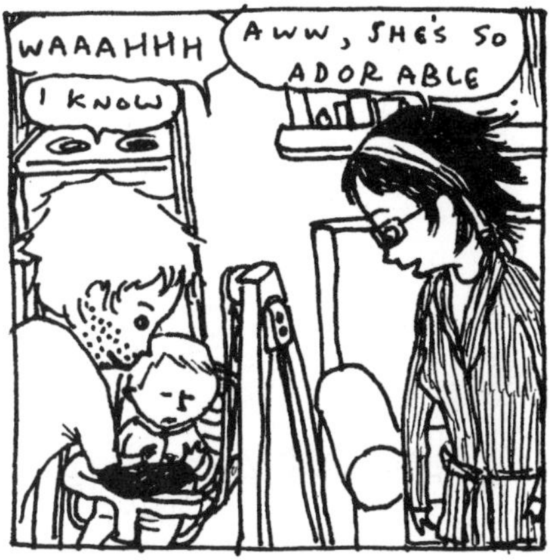
WAAAHHH
AWW, SHE'S SO ADORABLE
I KNOW

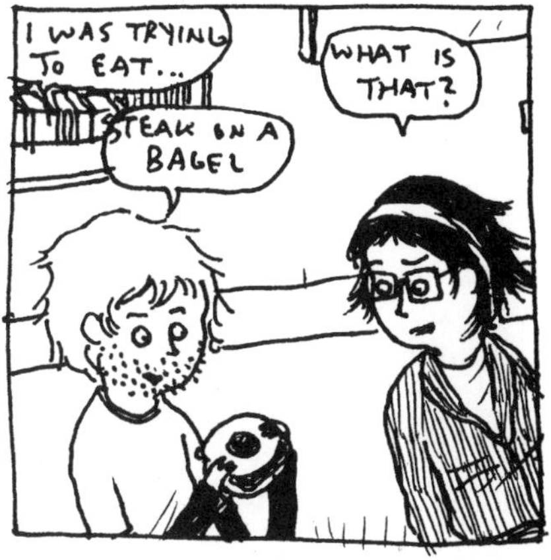
I WAS TRYING TO EAT...
WHAT IS THAT?
STEAK ON A BAGEL

WAAAHHHHHH
MAYBE SHE NEEDS HER DIAPER CHANGED

THAT WASN'T SO HARD... I'VE NEVER CHANGED A DIAPER BEFORE.
AT LEAST IT WASN'T POOPY...

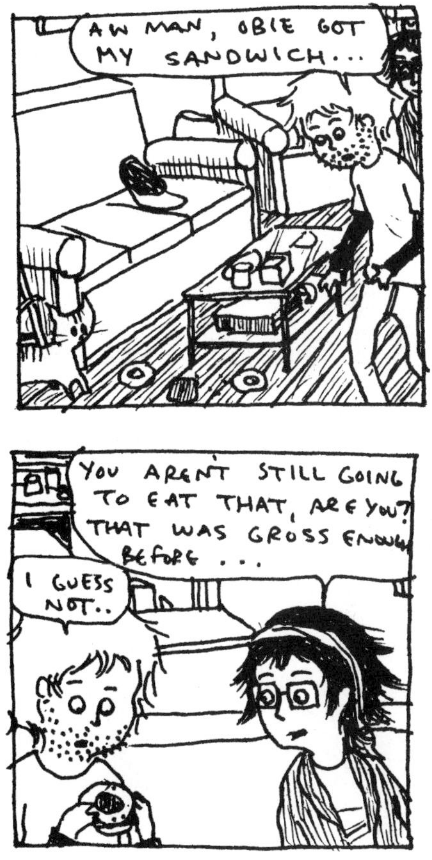
AW MAN, OBIE GOT MY SANDWICH...
YOU AREN'T STILL GOING TO EAT THAT, ARE YOU? THAT WAS GROSS ENOUGH BEFORE...
I GUESS NOT..

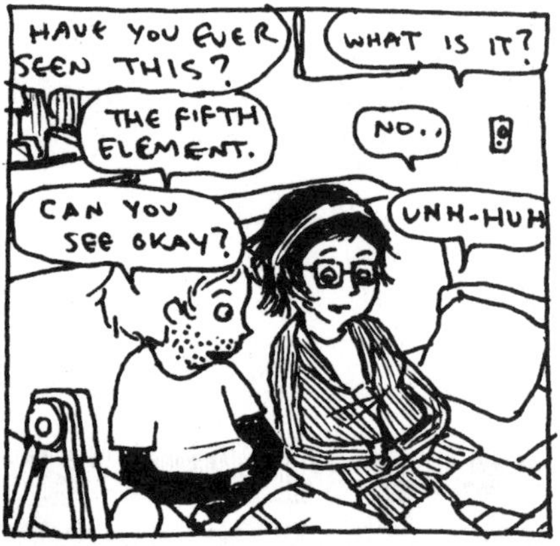
HAVE YOU EVER SEEN THIS?
WHAT IS IT?
THE FIFTH ELEMENT.
NO..
CAN YOU SEE OKAY?
UNH-HUH

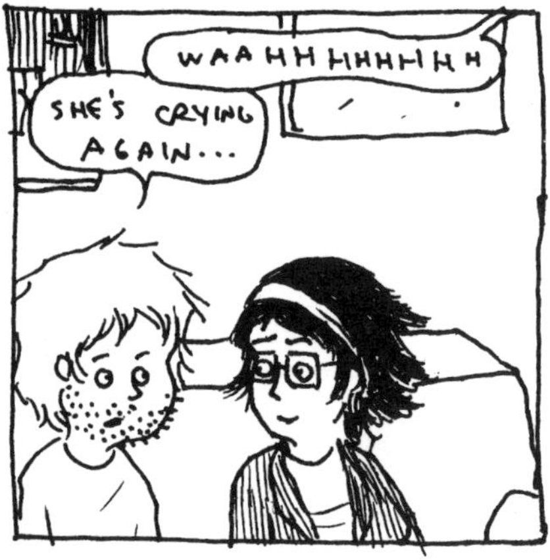
WAAHHHHHHHH
SHE'S CRYING AGAIN...

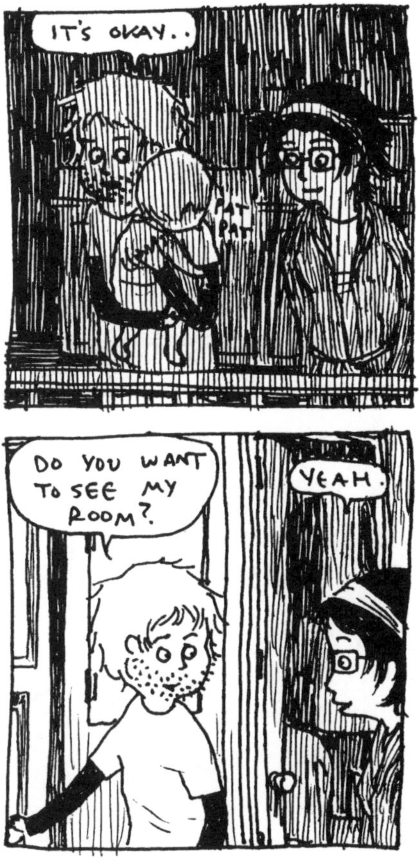
IT'S OKAY..
PAT PAT
DO YOU WANT TO SEE MY ROOM?
YEAH.

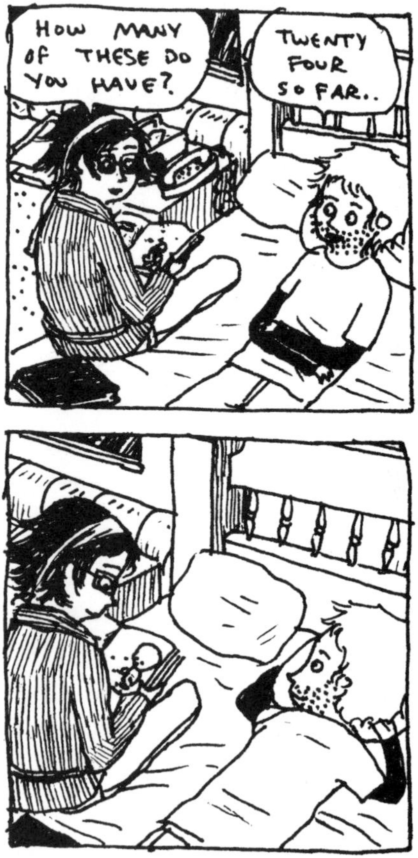
HOW MANY OF THESE DO YOU HAVE?
TWENTY FOUR SO FAR..

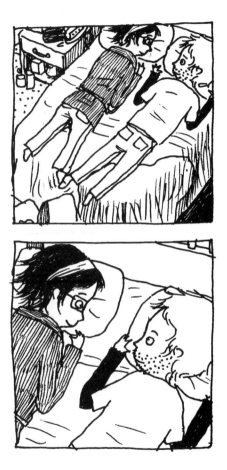

SLEEP WITH YOU

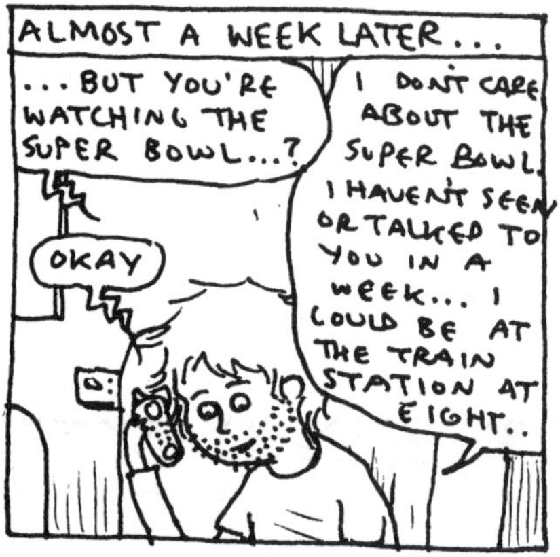
ALMOST A WEEK LATER...
...BUT YOU'RE WATCHING THE SUPER BOWL...?
I DON'T CARE ABOUT THE SUPER BOWL. I HAVEN'T SEEN OR TALKED TO YOU IN A WEEK... I COULD BE AT THE TRAIN STATION AT EIGHT..
OKAY

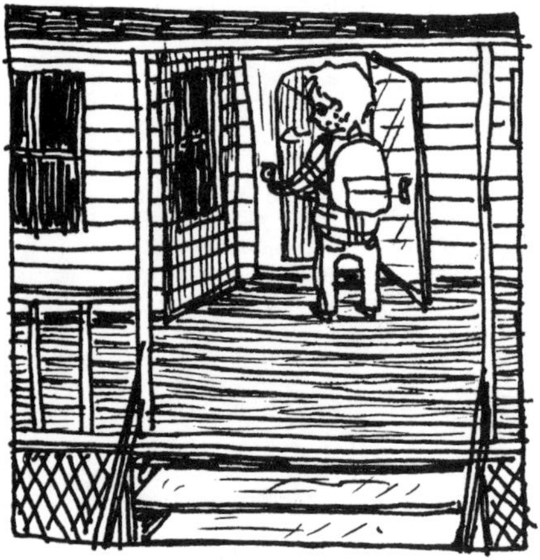

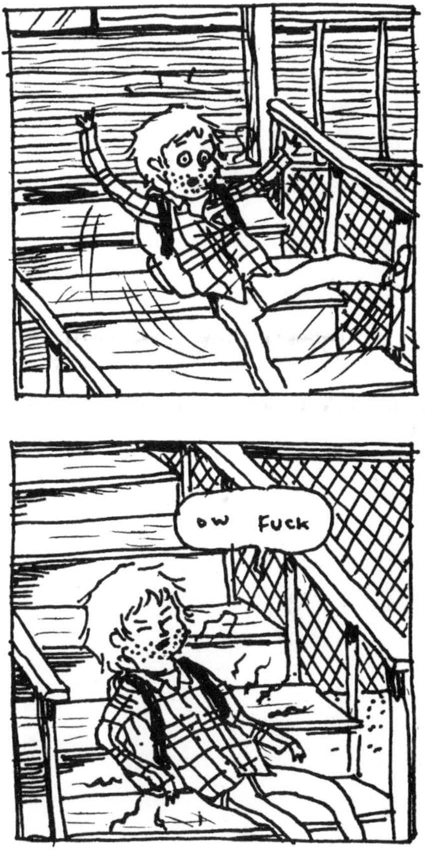
OW FUCK

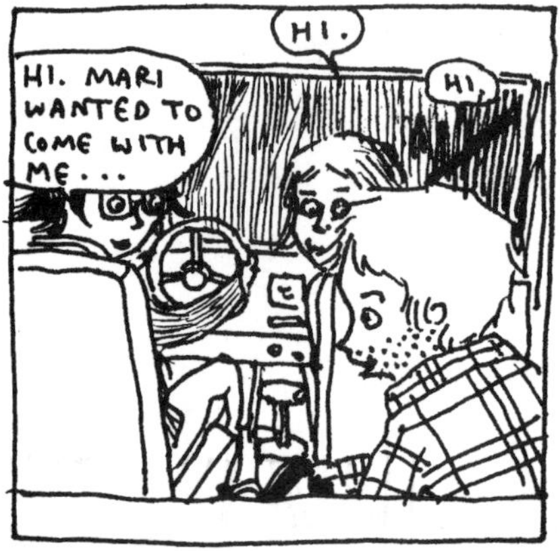
HI. MARI WANTED TO COME WITH ME...
HI.
HI.

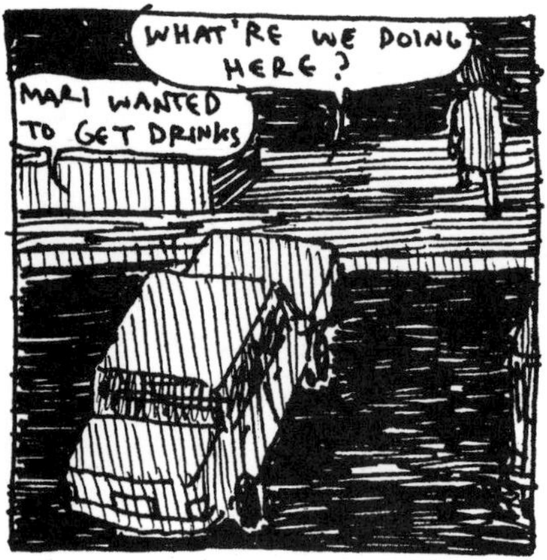
WHAT'RE WE DOING HERE?
MARI WANTED TO GET DRINKS

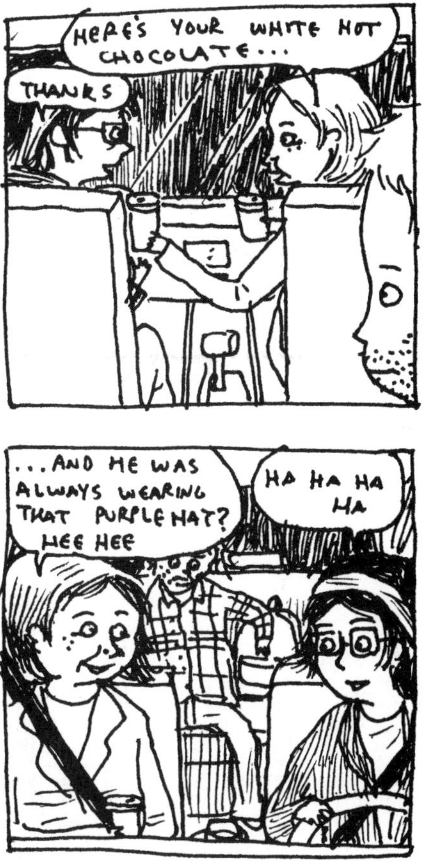
HERE'S YOUR WHITE HOT CHOCOLATE...
THANKS
...AND HE WAS ALWAYS WEARING THAT PURPLE HAT? HEE HEE
HA HA HA HA

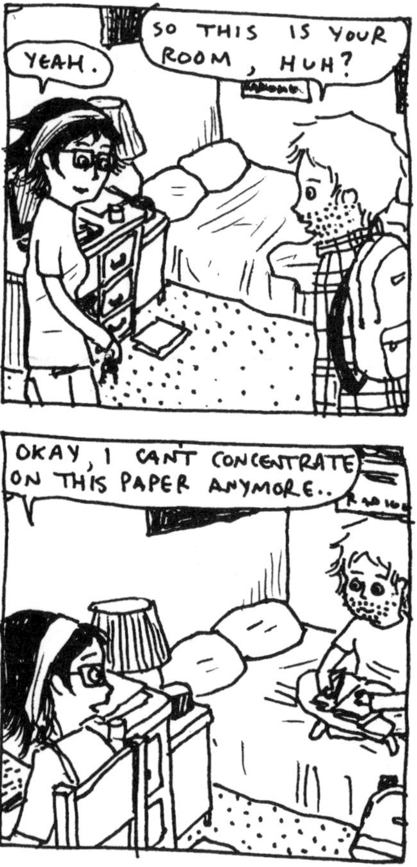
SO THIS IS YOUR ROOM, HUH?
YEAH.
OKAY, I CAN'T CONCENTRATE ON THIS PAPER ANYMORE..

SO YOU'VE HAD SEX WITH TWO GIRLS?
YEAH.
I'VE ONLY HAD SEX ONCE... WELL, I DON'T REALLY COUNT IT, SINCE...
YEAH... I KNOW...

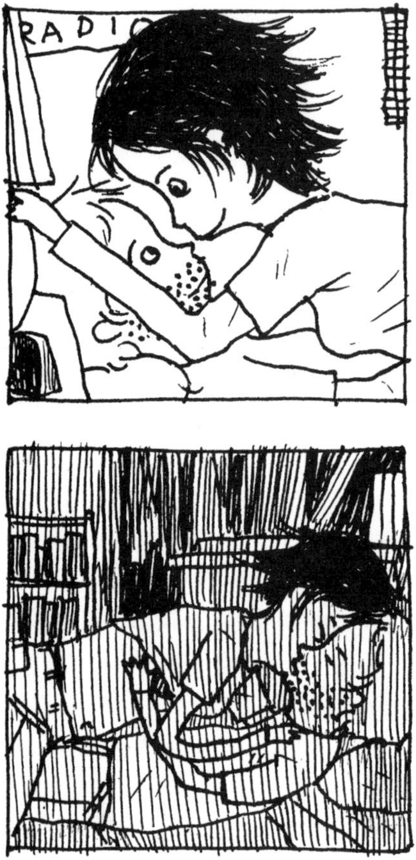
RADI

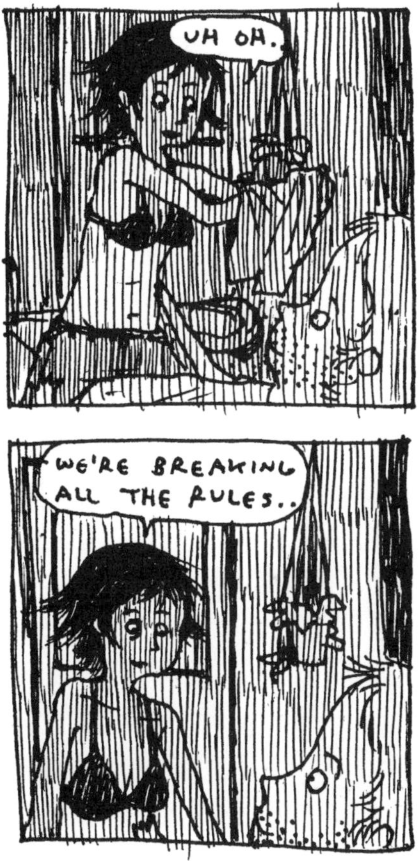
UH OH.
WE'RE BREAKING ALL THE RULES..

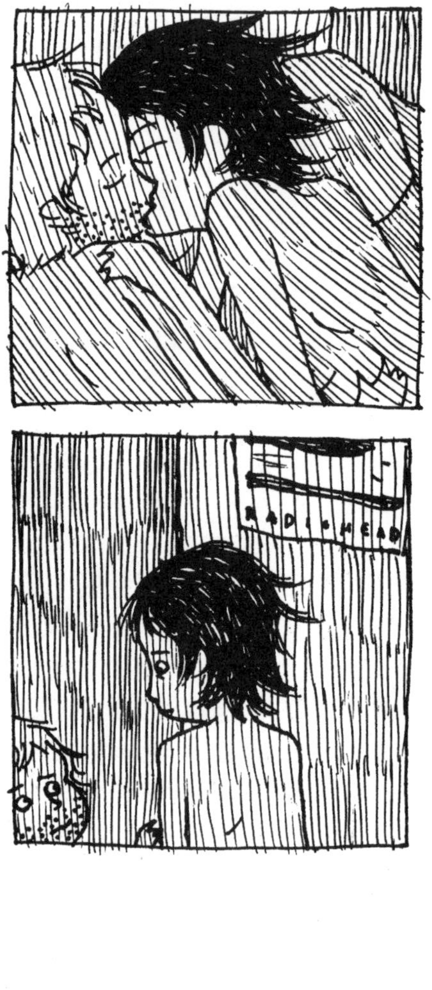
RADIOHEAD

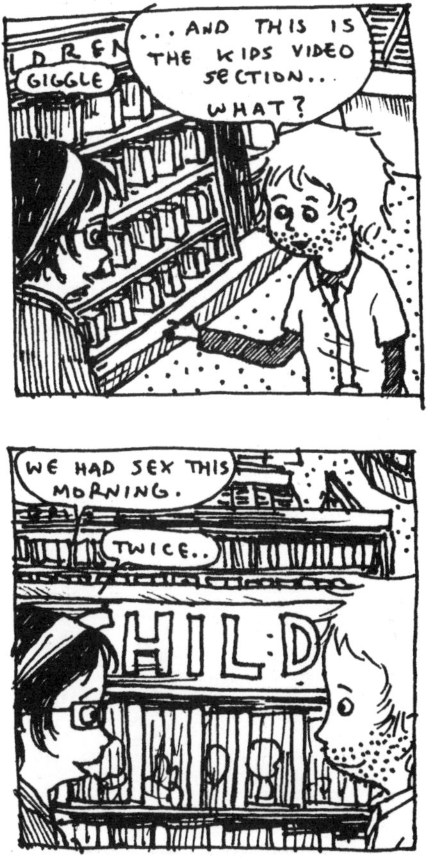
...AND THIS IS THE KIDS VIDEO SECTION... WHAT?
GIGGLE
WE HAD SEX THIS MORNING.
TWICE..
HILD

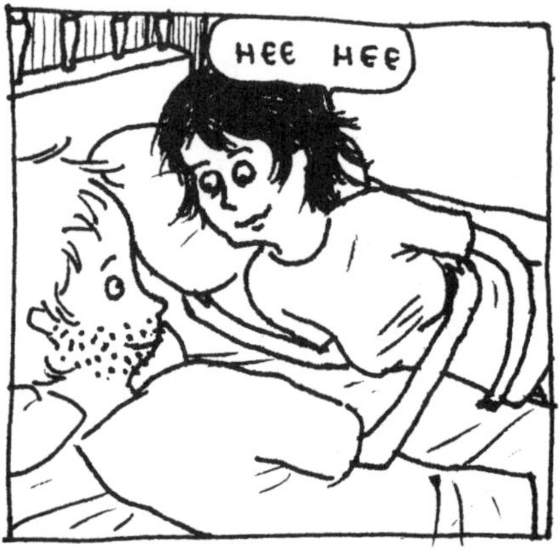
HEE HEE

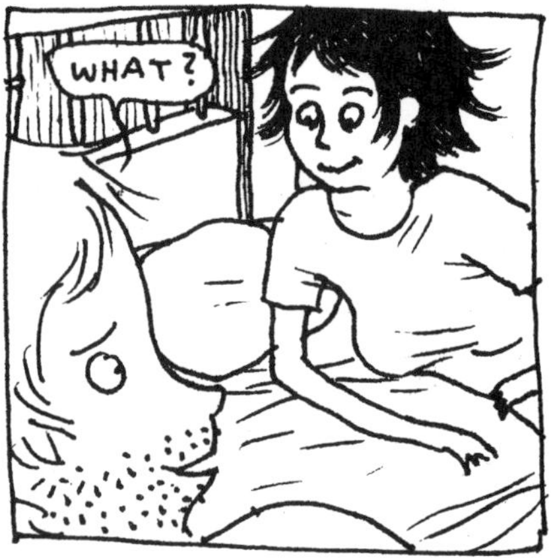
WHAT?

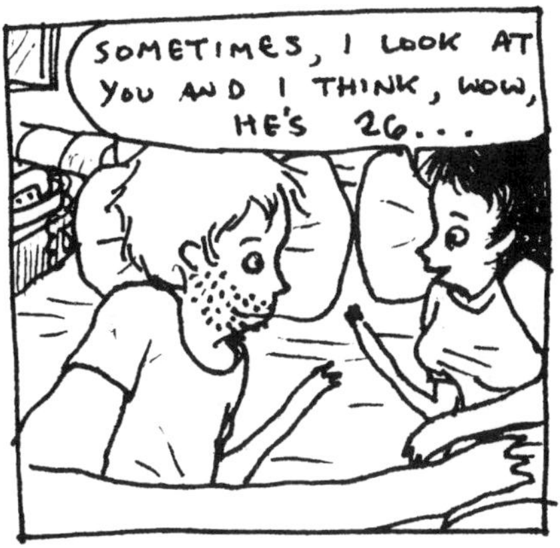
SOMETIMES, I LOOK AT YOU AND I THINK, WOW, HE'S 26...

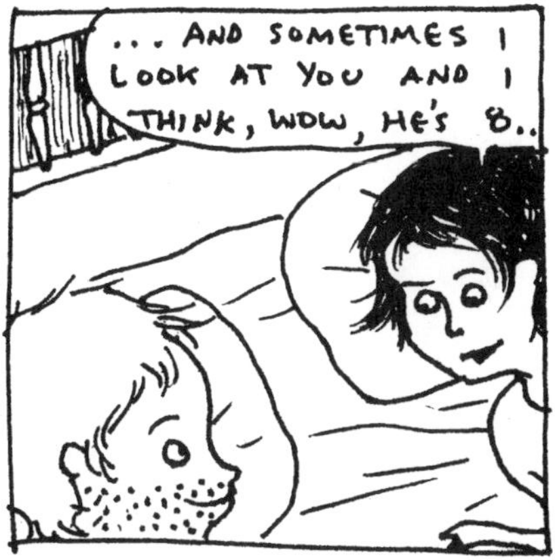
...AND SOMETIMES I LOOK AT YOU AND I THINK, WOW, HE'S 8..

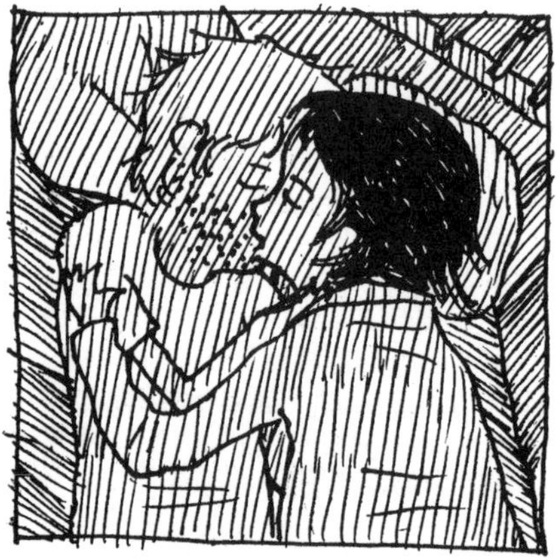
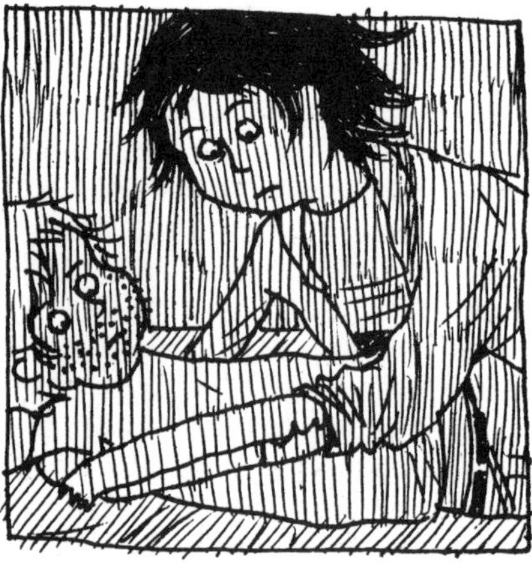

TOLD YOU I HAVE ISSUES..

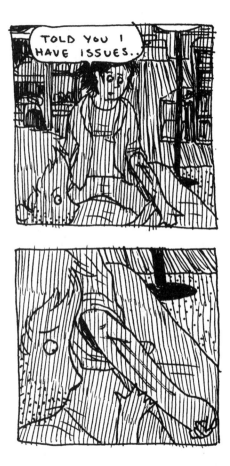

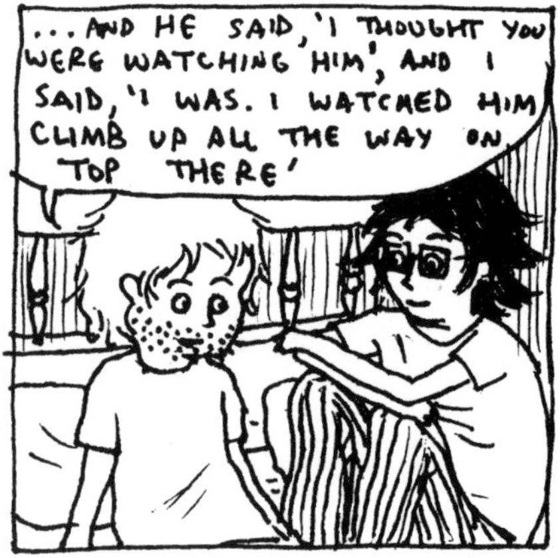
...AND HE SAID, 'I THOUGHT YOU WERE WATCHING HIM', AND I SAID, 'I WAS. I WATCHED HIM CLIMB UP ALL THE WAY ON TOP THERE'

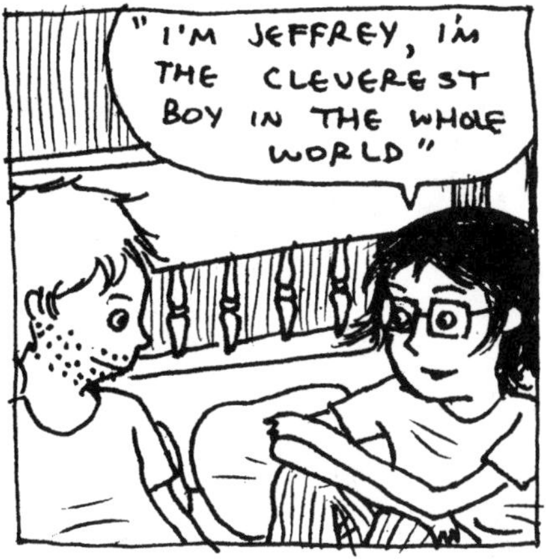
"I'M JEFFREY, I'M THE CLEVEREST BOY IN THE WHOLE WORLD"

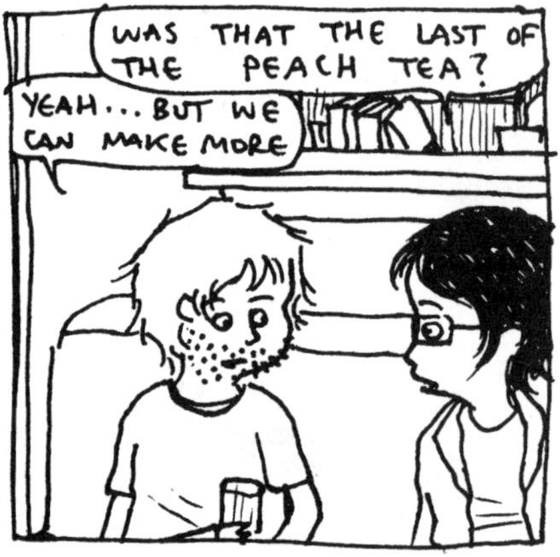
WAS THAT THE LAST OF THE PEACH TEA?
YEAH... BUT WE CAN MAKE MORE

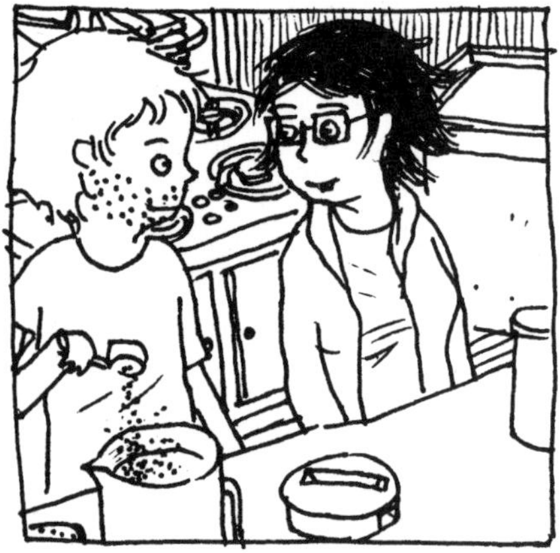

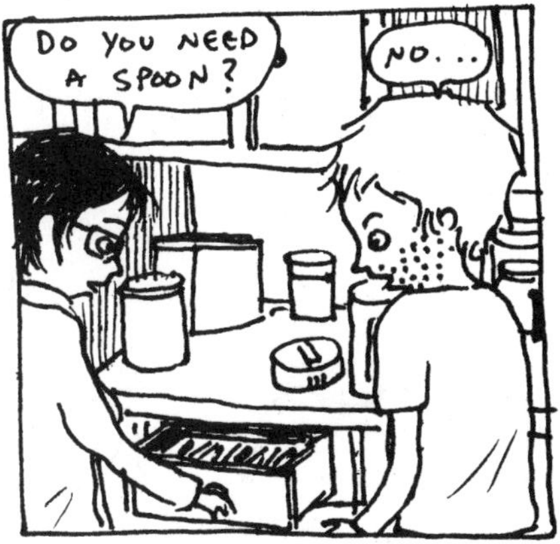
DO YOU NEED A SPOON?
NO...

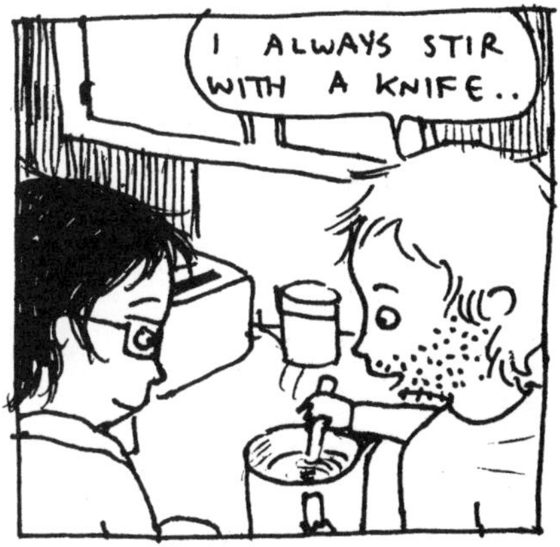
I ALWAYS STIR WITH A KNIFE..

I WAS DYING LAUGHING BEHIND THE PANTS

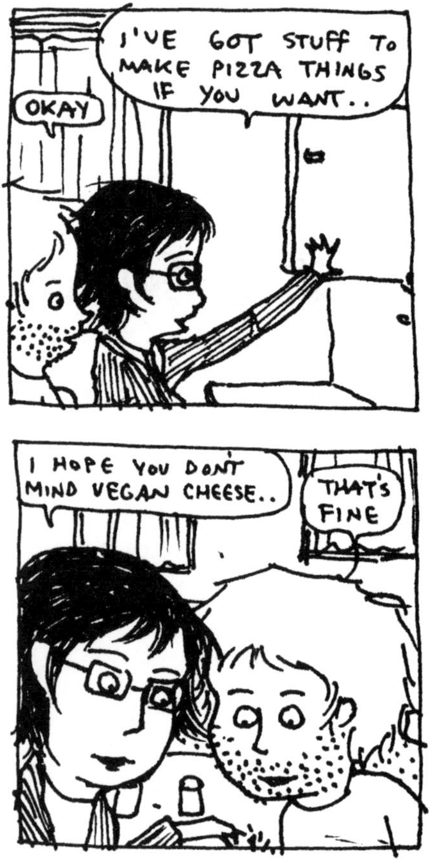
I'VE GOT STUFF TO MAKE PIZZA THINGS IF YOU WANT..
OKAY
I HOPE YOU DON'T MIND VEGAN CHEESE..
THAT'S FINE

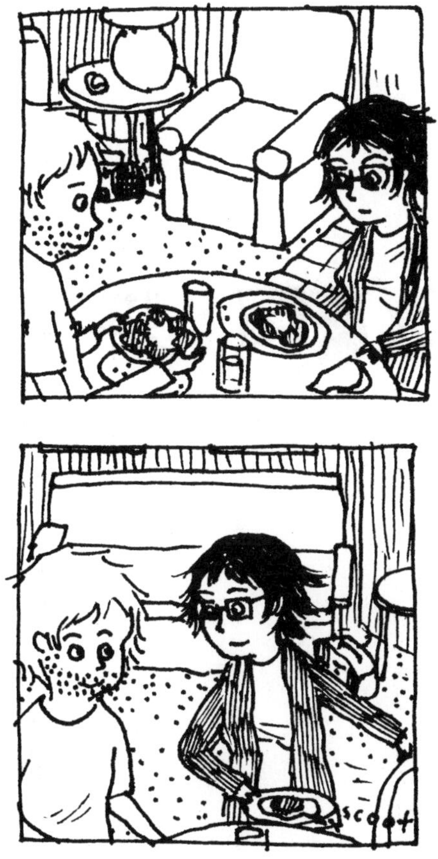
scoot

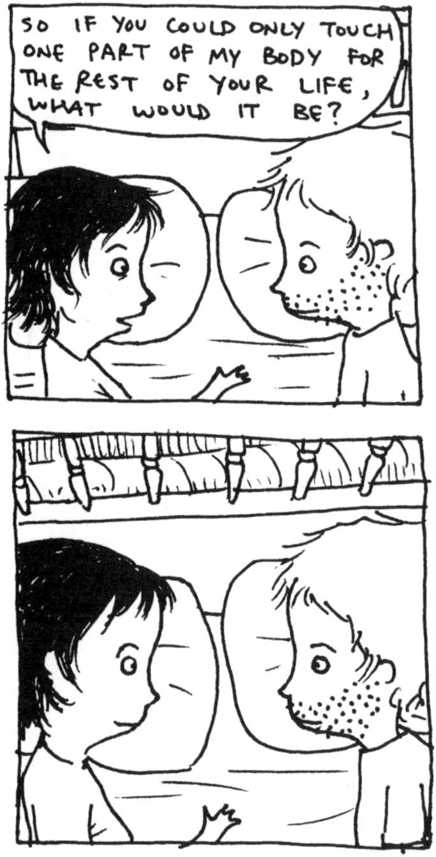
SO IF YOU COULD ONLY TOUCH ONE PART OF MY BODY FOR THE REST OF YOUR LIFE, WHAT WOULD IT BE?

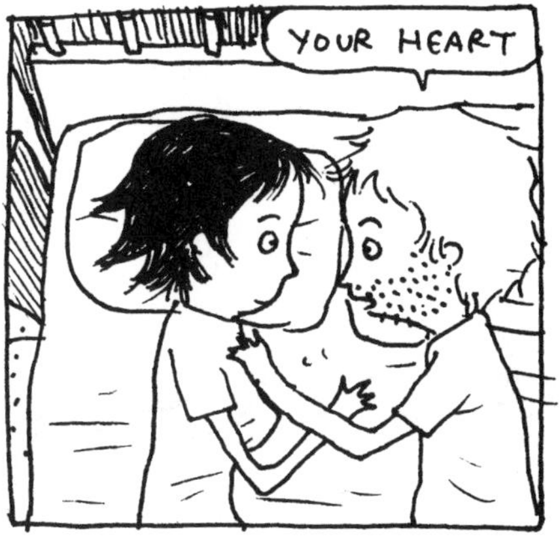
YOUR HEART

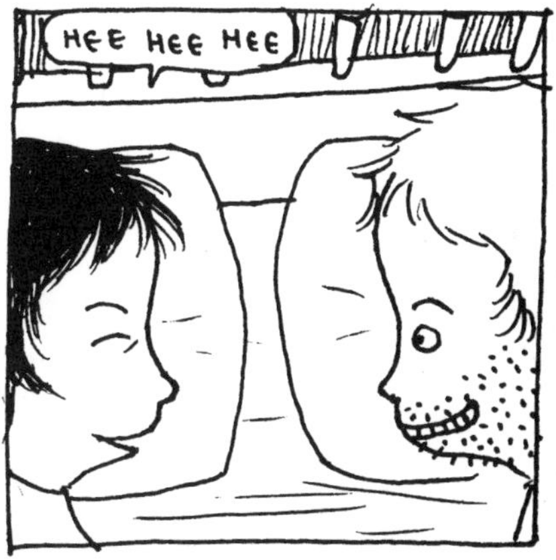
HEE HEE HEE

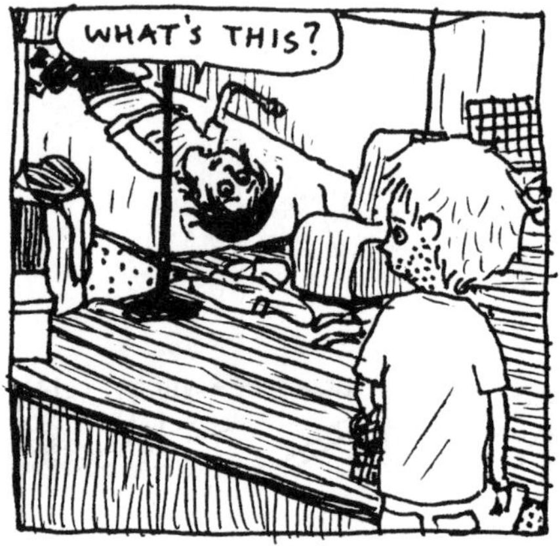
WHAT'S THIS?

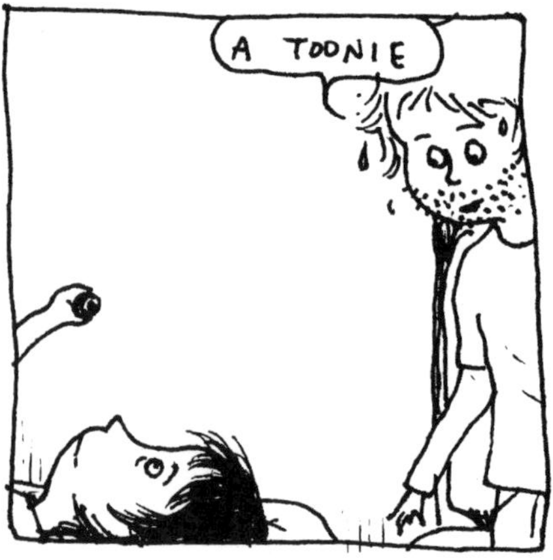
A TOONIE

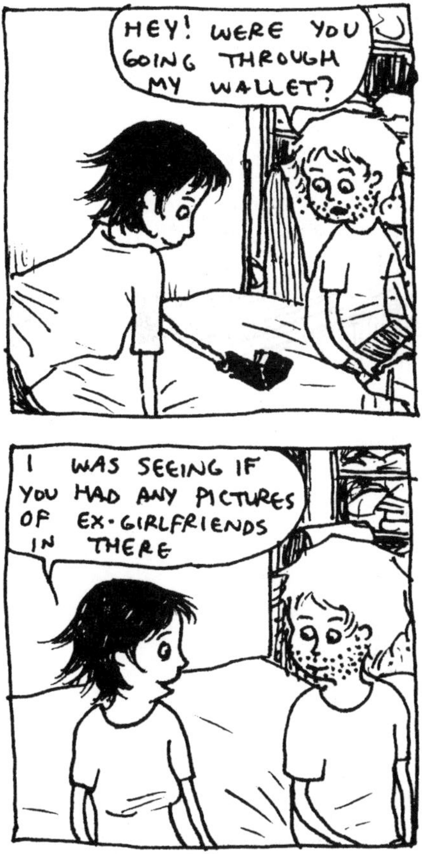
HEY! WERE YOU GOING THROUGH MY WALLET?
I WAS SEEING IF YOU HAD ANY PICTURES OF EX-GIRLFRIENDS IN THERE

PRETTINESS

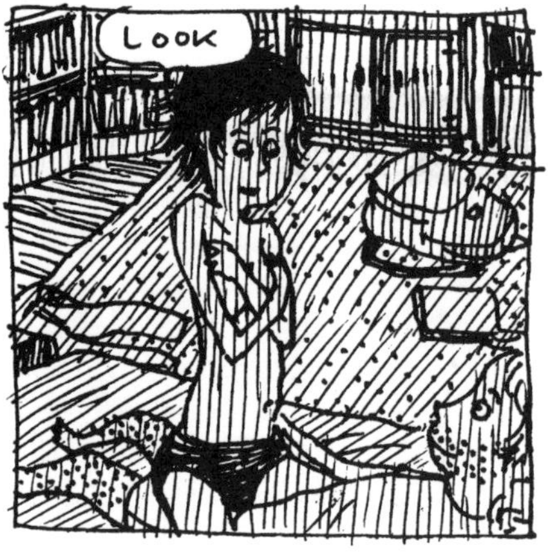
LOOK

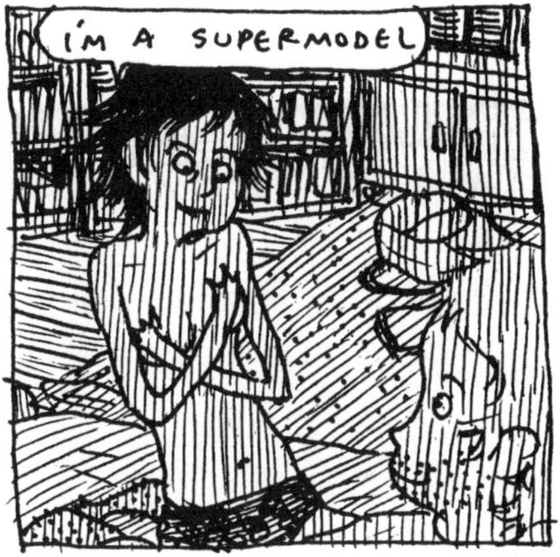
I'M A SUPERMODEL

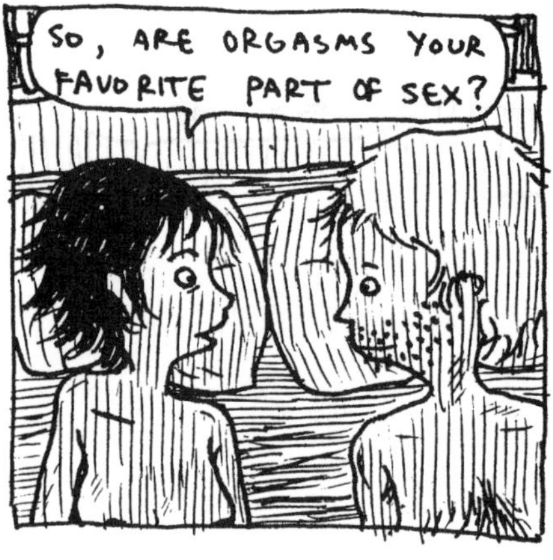
SO, ARE ORGASMS YOUR FAVORITE PART OF SEX?

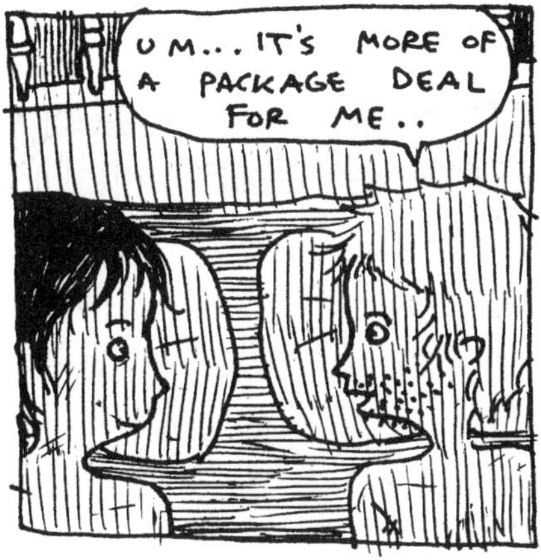
UM... IT'S MORE OF A PACKAGE DEAL FOR ME..

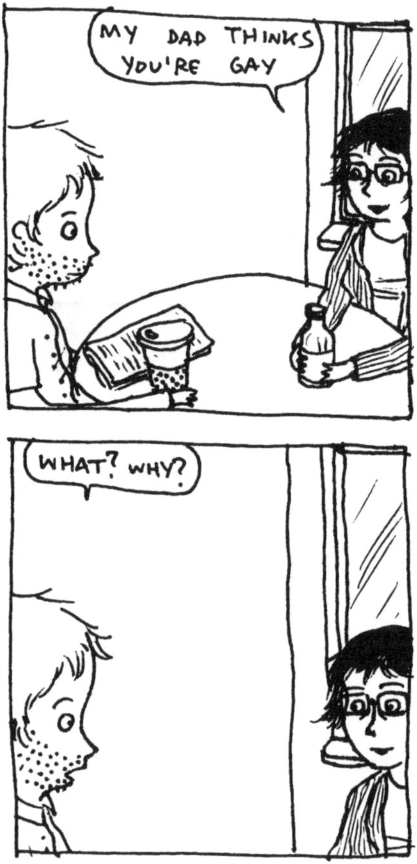
MY DAD THINKS YOU'RE GAY
WHAT? WHY?

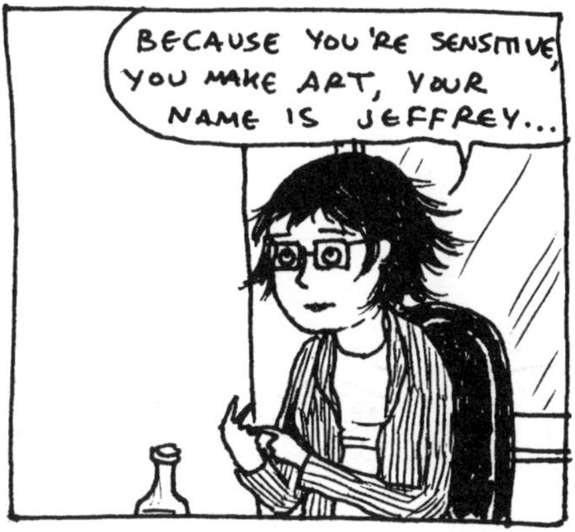
BECAUSE YOU'RE SENSITIVE, YOU MAKE ART, YOUR NAME IS JEFFREY...

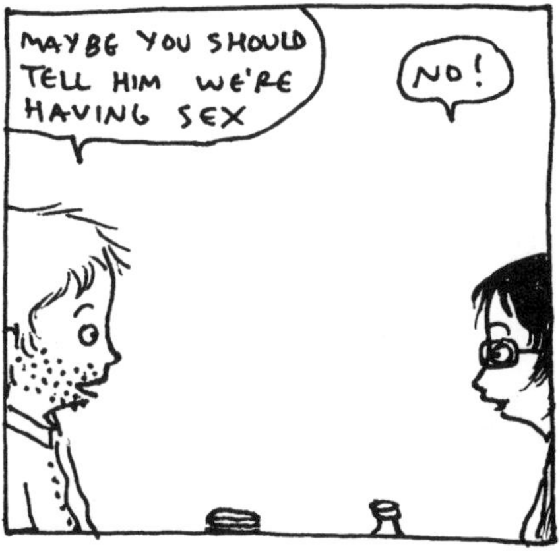
MAYBE YOU SHOULD TELL HIM WE'RE HAVING SEX
NO!

GRASS IS GREENER

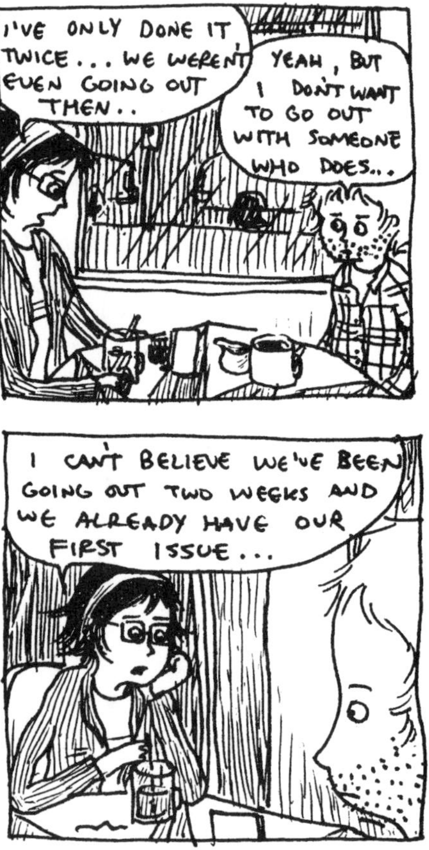
I'VE ONLY DONE IT TWICE... WE WEREN'T EVEN GOING OUT THEN..
YEAH, BUT I DON'T WANT TO GO OUT WITH SOMEONE WHO DOES...
I CAN'T BELIEVE WE'VE BEEN GOING OUT TWO WEEKS AND WE ALREADY HAVE OUR FIRST ISSUE...

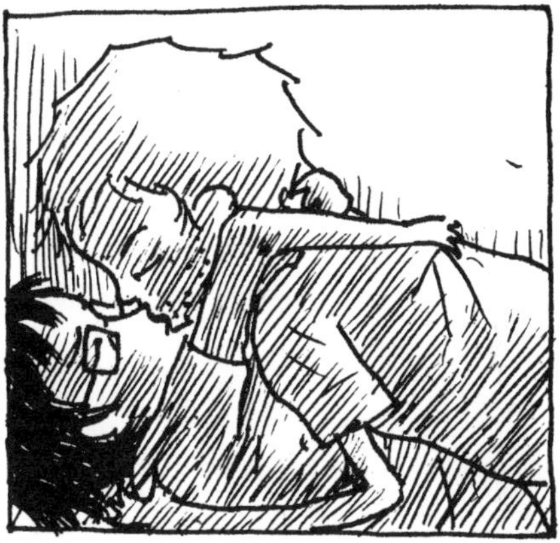

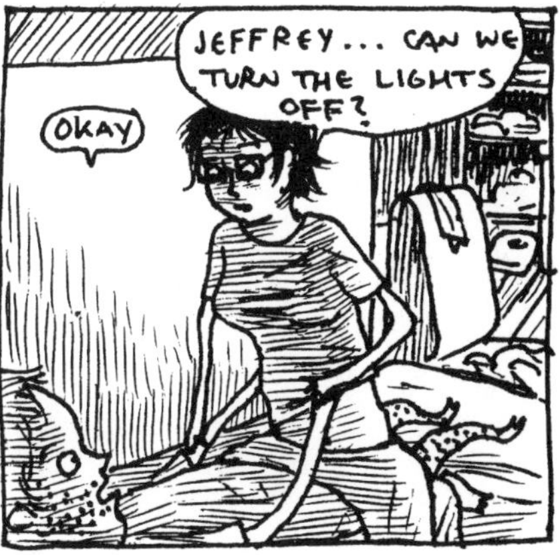
JEFFREY... CAN WE TURN THE LIGHTS OFF?
OKAY

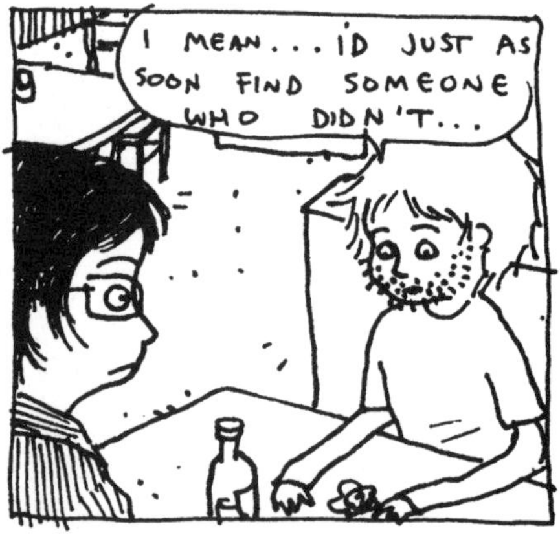
I MEAN... ID JUST AS SOON FIND SOMEONE WHO DIDN'T...

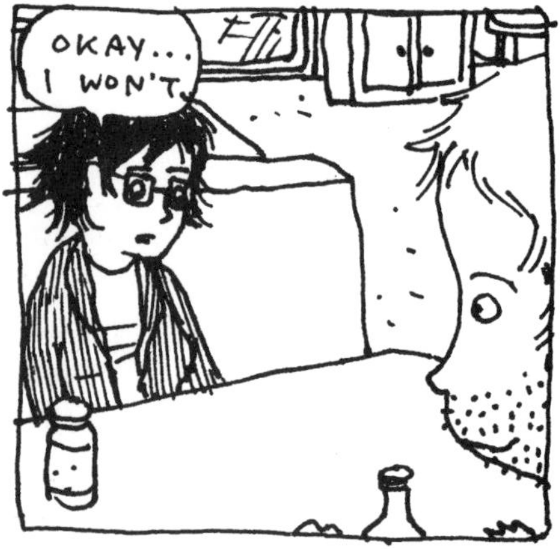
OKAY... I WON'T.

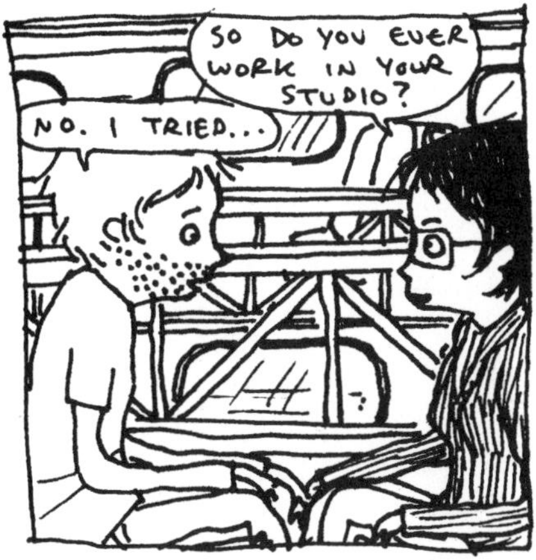
SO DO YOU EVER WORK IN YOUR STUDIO?
NO. I TRIED...

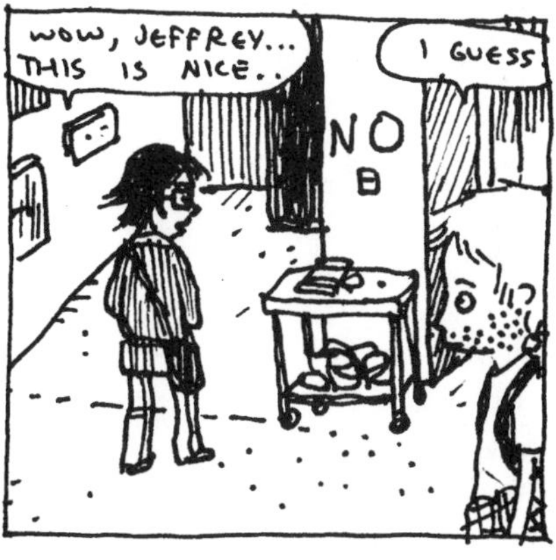
WOW, JEFFREY... THIS IS NICE..
I GUESS
NO
B

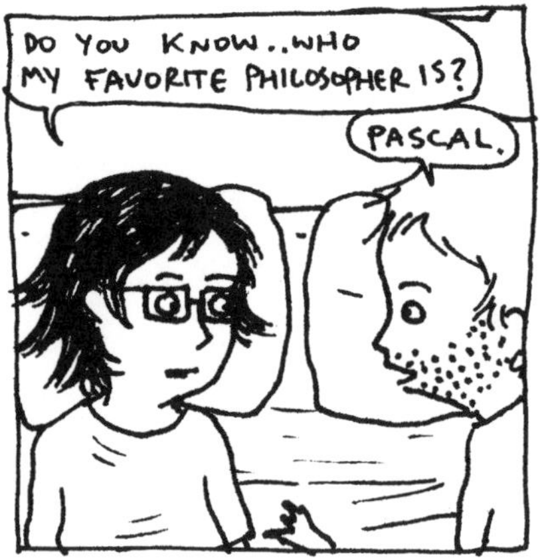
DO YOU KNOW..WHO MY FAVORITE PHILOSOPHER IS?
PASCAL.

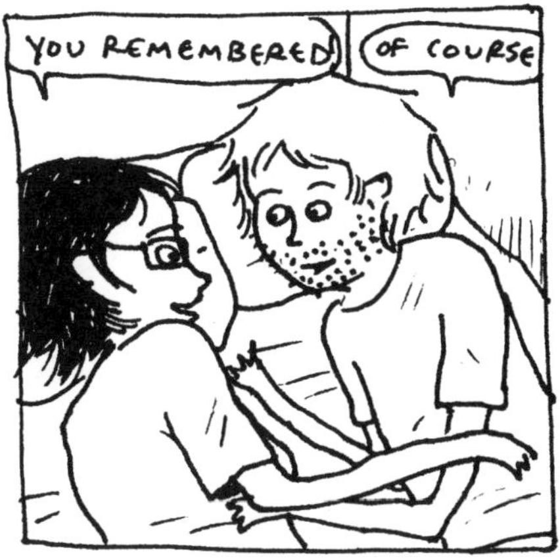
YOU REMEMBERED
OF COURSE

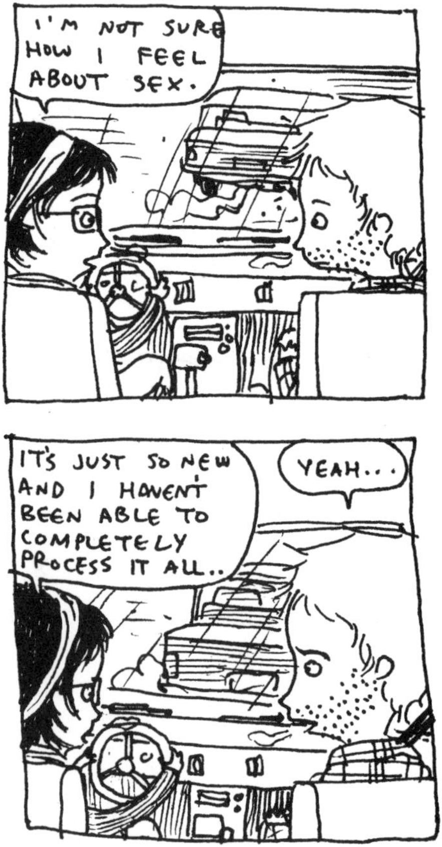
I'M NOT SURE HOW I FEEL ABOUT SEX.
IT'S JUST SO NEW AND I HAVEN'T BEEN ABLE TO COMPLETELY PROCESS IT ALL..
YEAH...

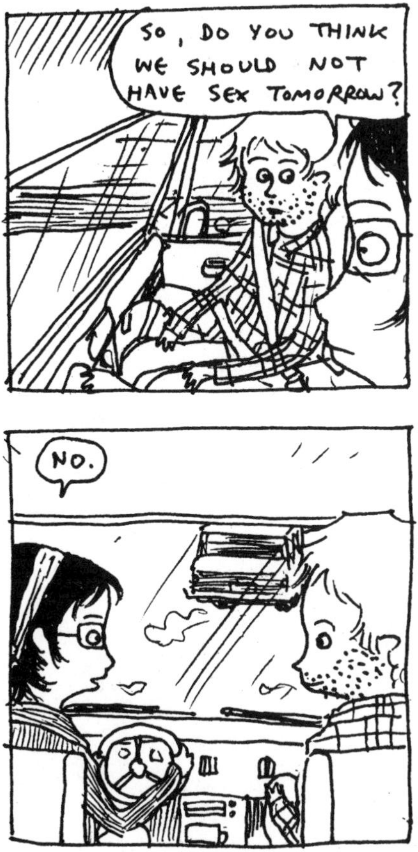
SO, DO YOU THINK WE SHOULD NOT HAVE SEX TOMORROW?
NO.

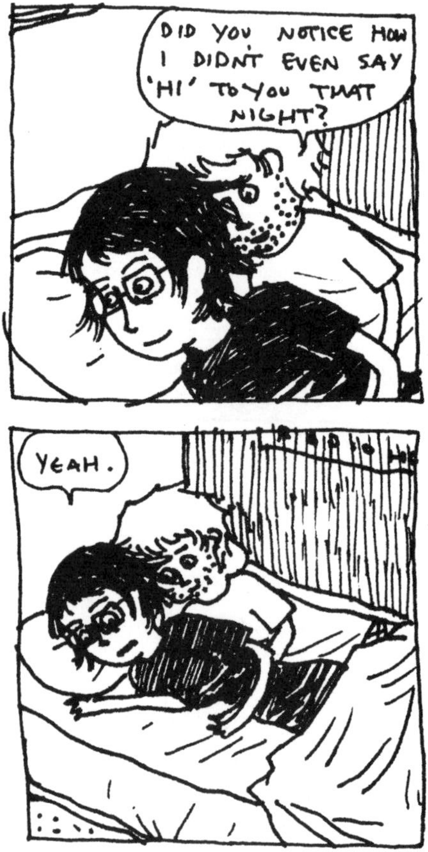
DID YOU NOTICE HOW I DIDN'T EVEN SAY 'HI' TO YOU THAT NIGHT?
YEAH.

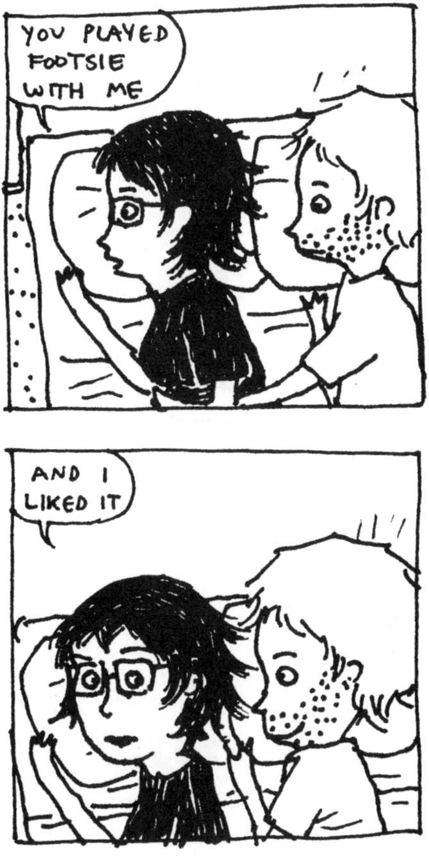
YOU PLAYED FOOTSIE WITH ME
AND I LIKED IT

BETWEEN LOVERS

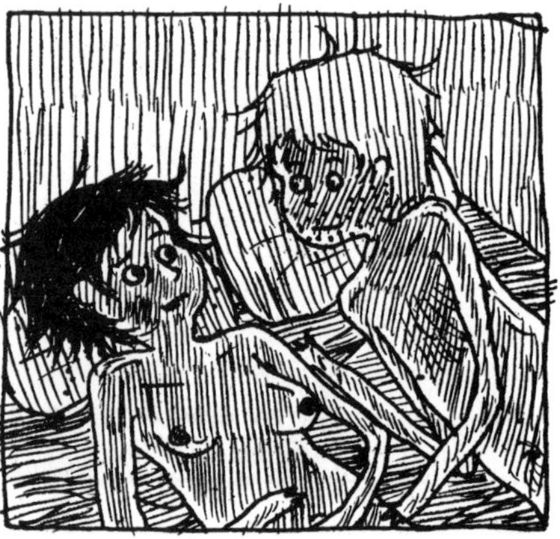

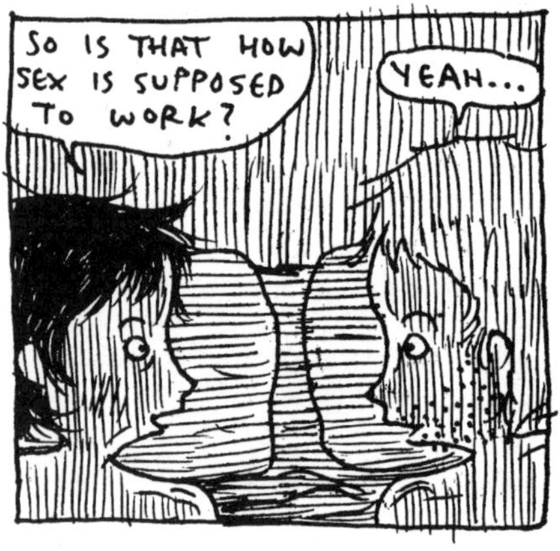
SO IS THAT HOW SEX IS SUPPOSED TO WORK?
YEAH...

SO.. WHEN YOU HAD SEX WITH - EWWWW!
WHAT?
EWWW, SEX WITH ME IS GROSS?
NO, THINKING ABOUT YOU HAVING SEX WITH OTHER GIRLS IS GROSS

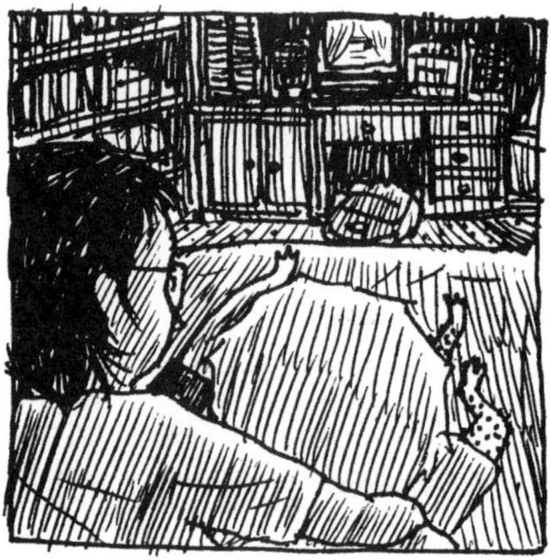

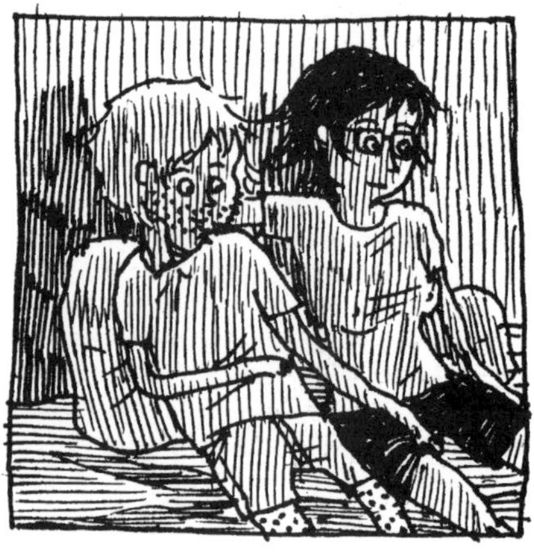

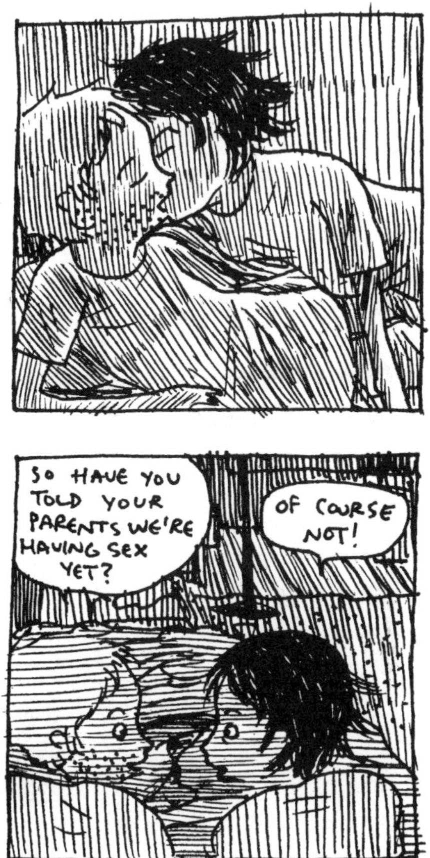
SO HAVE YOU TOLD YOUR PARENTS WE'RE HAVING SEX YET?
OF COURSE NOT!

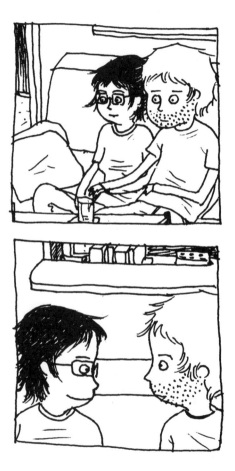

MMM
MMMPH
M
I LIKE PASSIONATE BOUTS OF KISSING

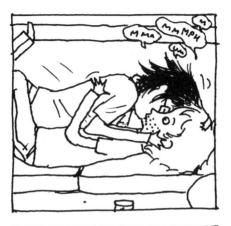

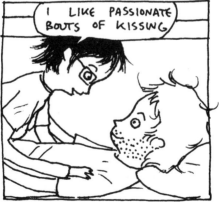

FEBRUARY

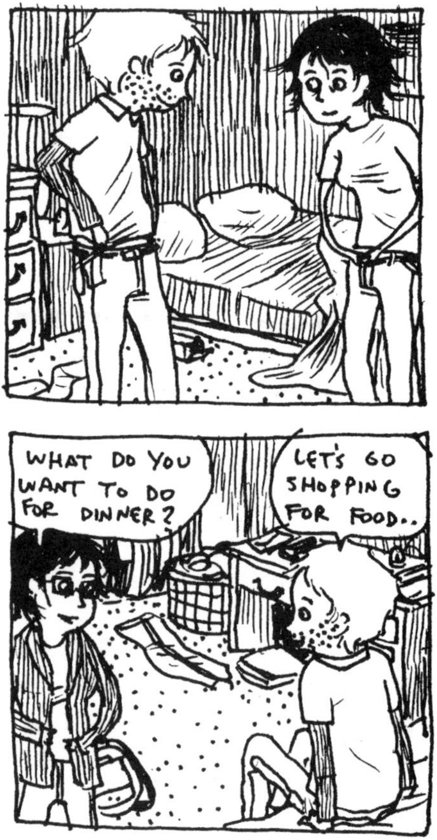
WHAT DO YOU WANT TO DO FOR DINNER?
LET'S GO SHOPPING FOR FOOD..

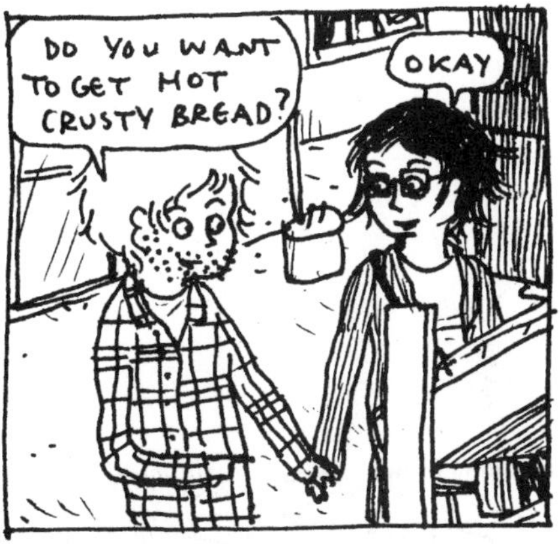
DO YOU WANT TO GET HOT CRUSTY BREAD?
OKAY

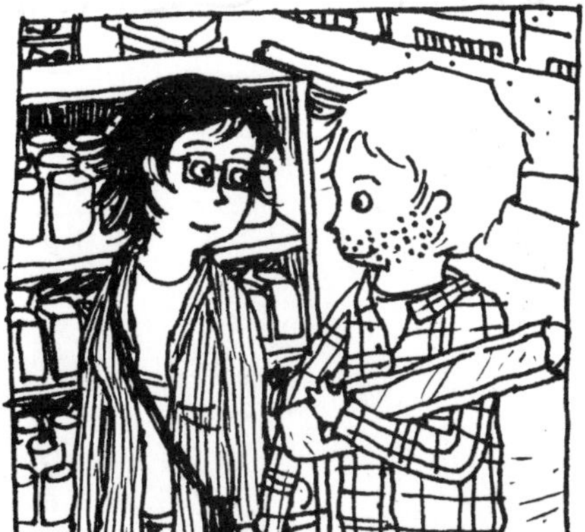

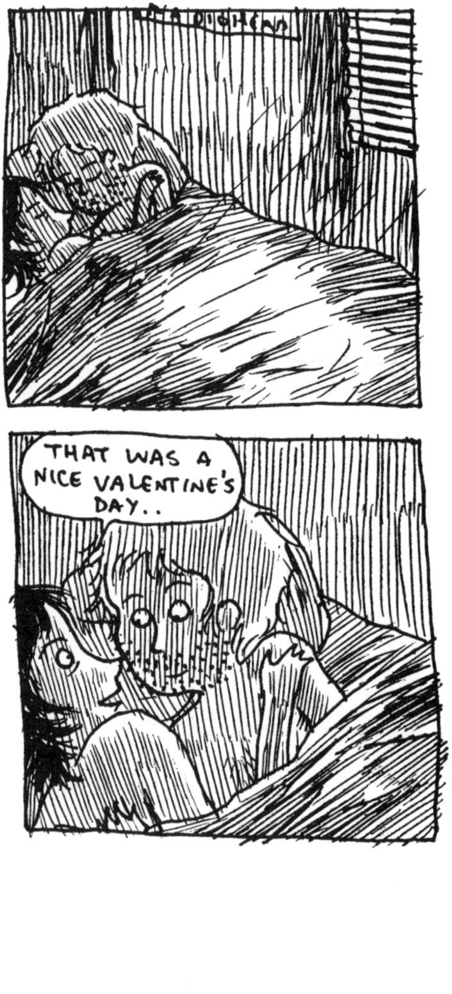
THAT WAS A NICE VALENTINE'S DAY..

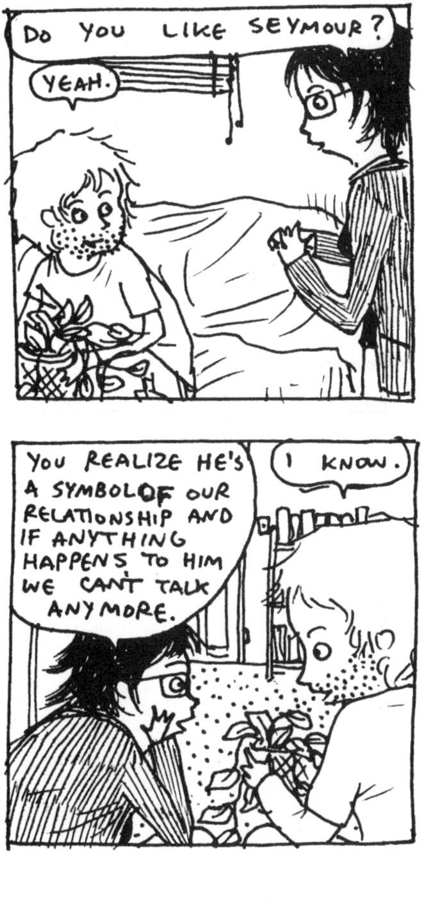
DO YOU LIKE SEYMOUR?
YEAH.
YOU REALIZE HE'S A SYMBOL OF OUR RELATIONSHIP AND IF ANYTHING HAPPENS TO HIM WE CAN'T TALK ANYMORE.
I KNOW.

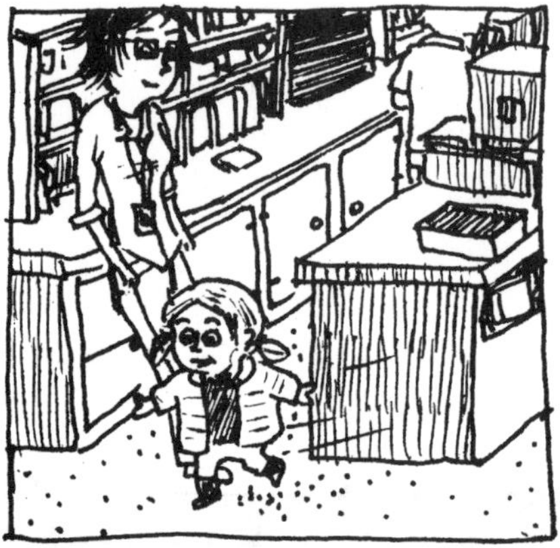

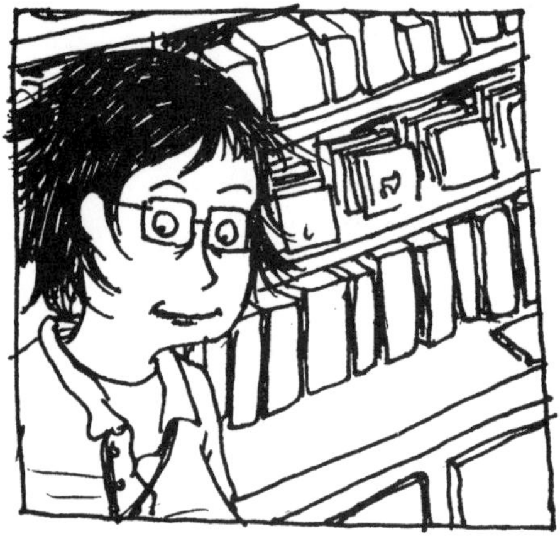

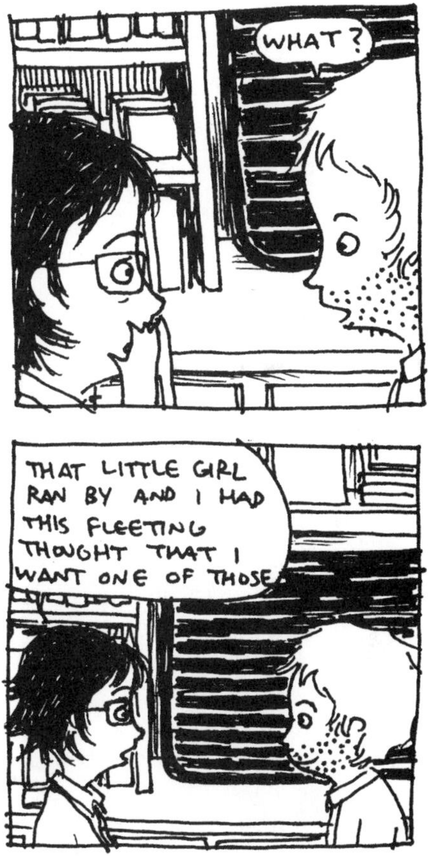
WHAT?
THAT LITTLE GIRL RAN BY AND I HAD THIS FLEETING THOUGHT THAT I WANT ONE OF THOSE

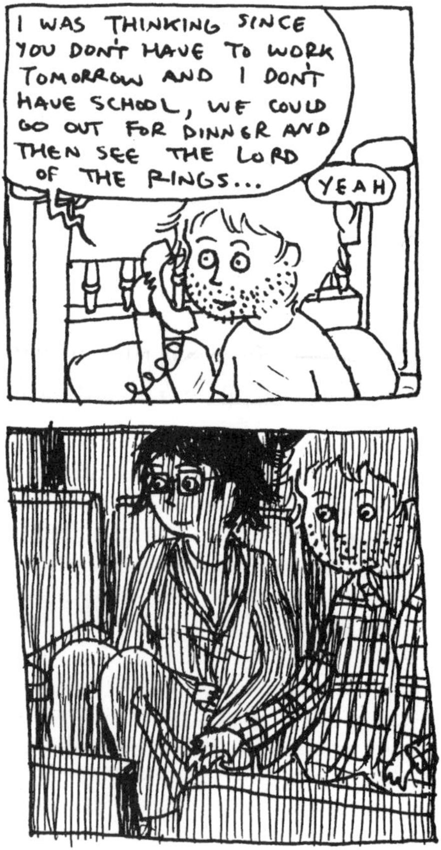
I WAS THINKING SINCE YOU DON'T HAVE TO WORK TOMORROW AND I DON'T HAVE SCHOOL, WE COULD GO OUT FOR DINNER AND THEN SEE THE LORD OF THE RINGS...
YEAH

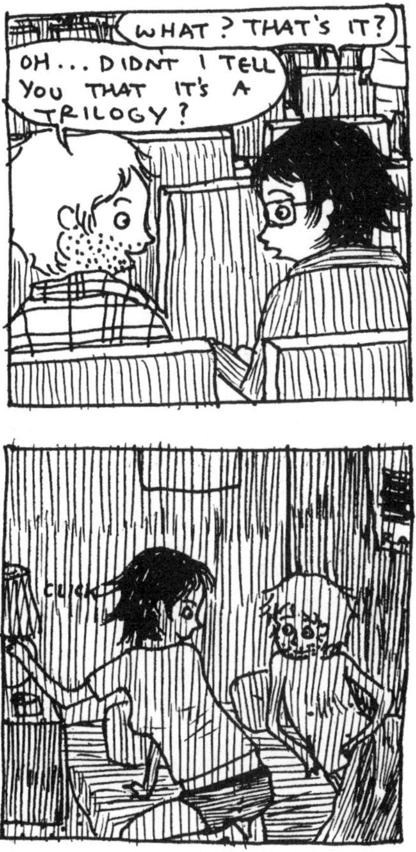
WHAT? THAT'S IT?
OH... DIDN'T I TELL YOU THAT IT'S A TRILOGY?
CLICK

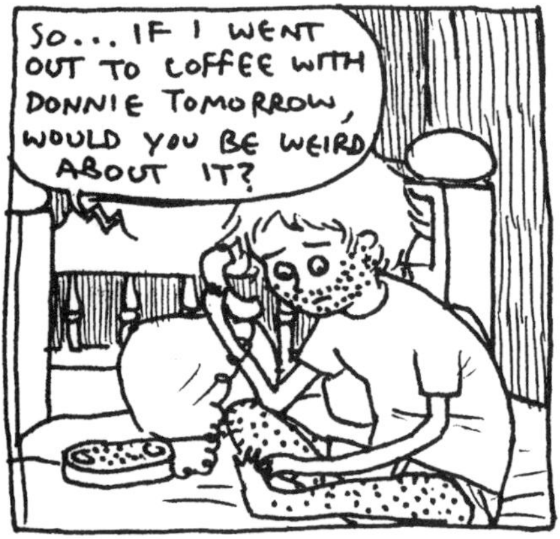
SO... IF I WENT OUT TO COFFEE WITH DONNIE TOMORROW, WOULD YOU BE WEIRD ABOUT IT?

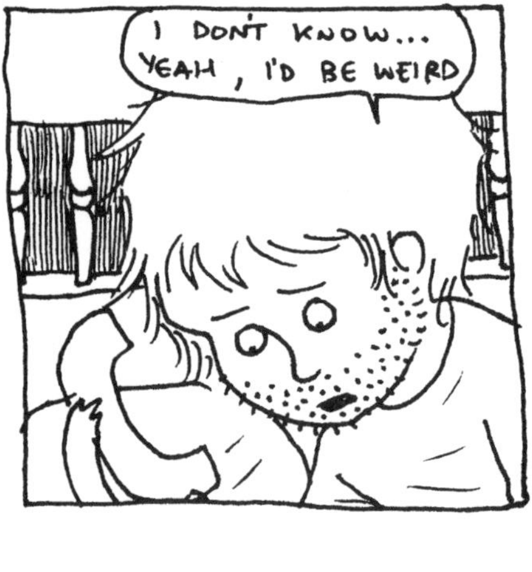
I DON'T KNOW... YEAH, I'D BE WEIRD

IT'S NOT LIKE A DATE. I DON'T WANT TO BE WITH HIM..
YEAH, BUT EVEN IF YOU'RE NOT PHYSICALLY INTIMATE THERE'S A LINE YOU CAN CROSS WITH EMOTIONAL INTIMACY...
WELL I'M NOT GOING TO BE INTIMATE WITH OTHER BOYS...
WELL I'M NOT GOING TO TELL YOU NOT TO GO TO COFFEE WITH HIM. I'M JUST SAYING I'LL PROBABLY BE WEIRD..

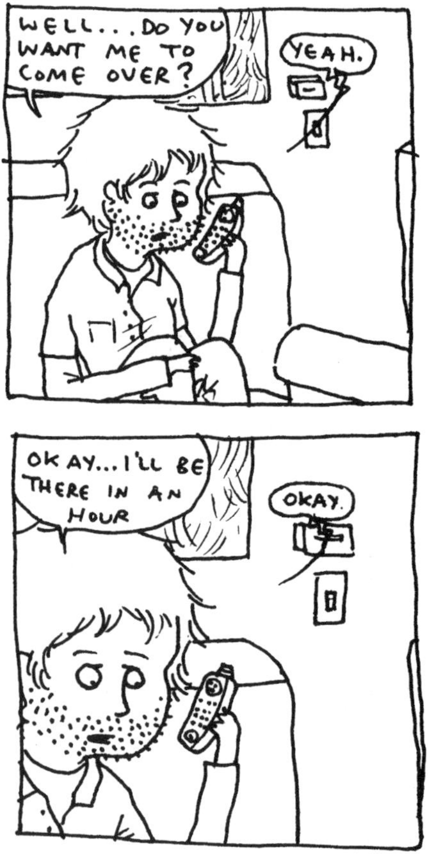
WELL...DO YOU WANT ME TO COME OVER?
YEAH.
OKAY...I'LL BE THERE IN AN HOUR
OKAY.

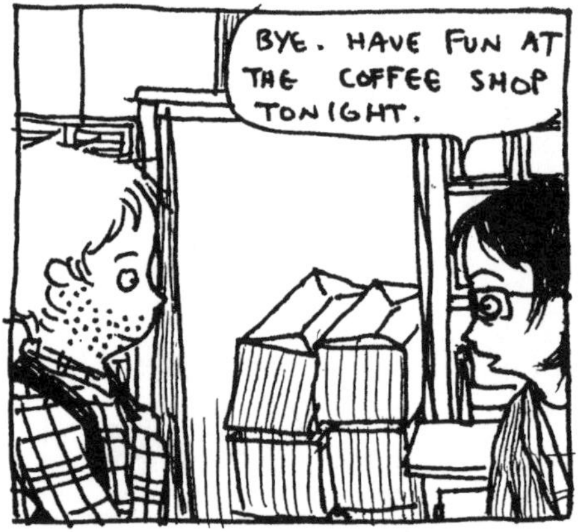
BYE. HAVE FUN AT THE COFFEE SHOP TONIGHT.

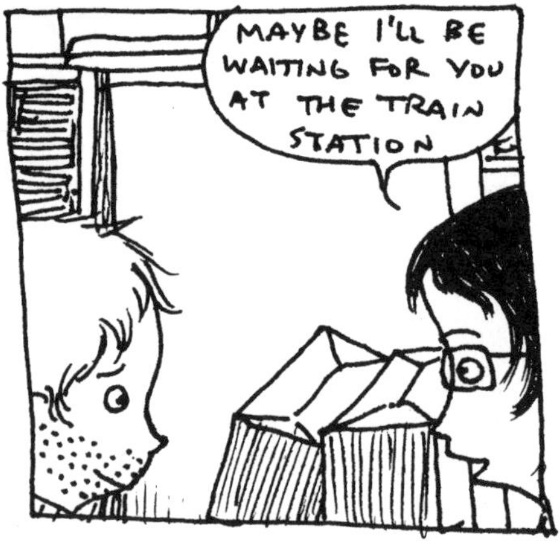
MAYBE I'LL BE WAITING FOR YOU AT THE TRAIN STATION

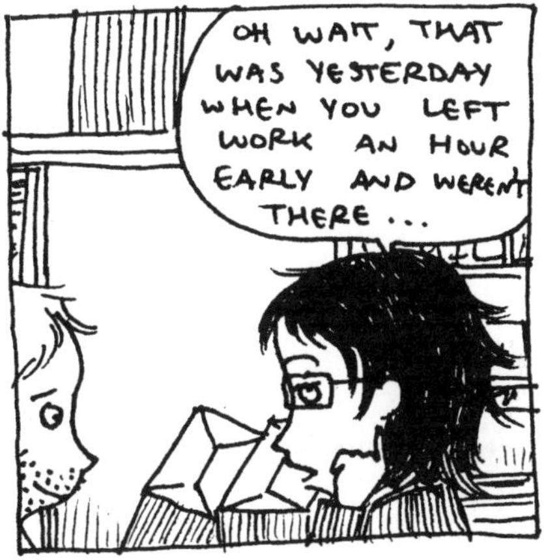
OH WAIT, THAT WAS YESTERDAY WHEN YOU LEFT WORK AN HOUR EARLY AND WEREN'T THERE...

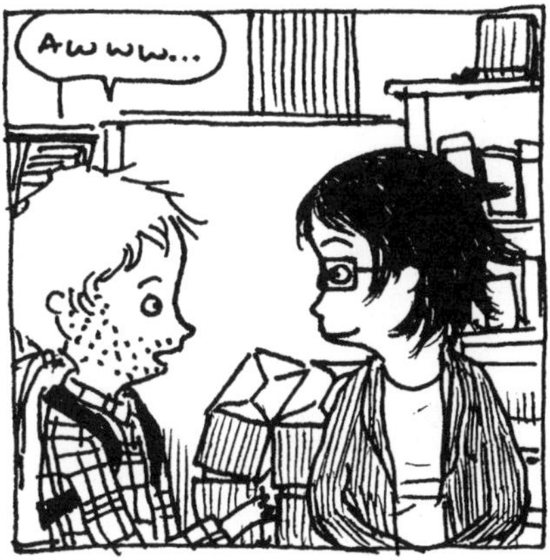
AWWW...

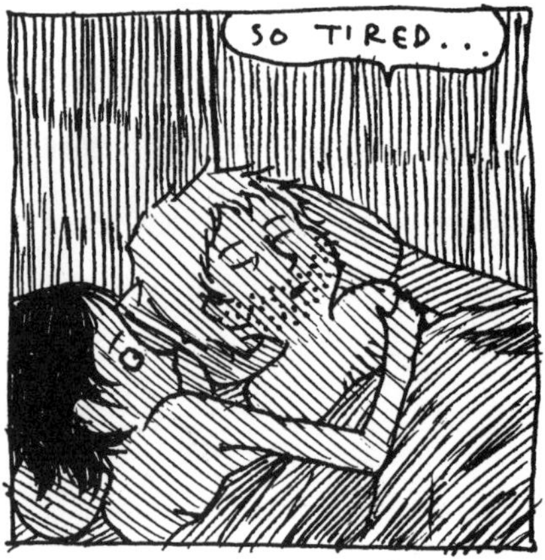
SO TIRED...

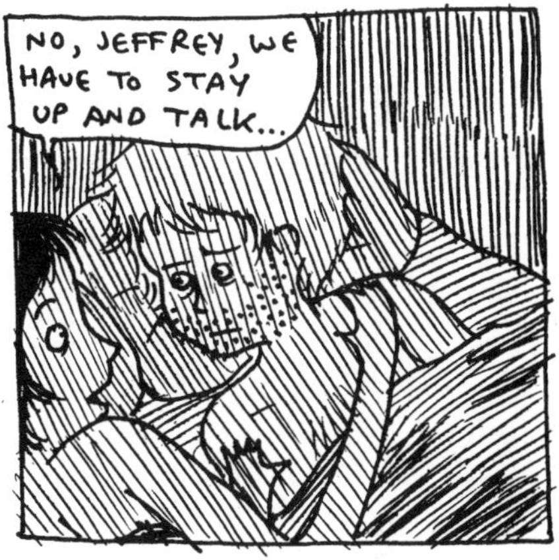
NO, JEFFREY, WE HAVE TO STAY UP AND TALK...

THE DIFFERENCE BETWEEN US

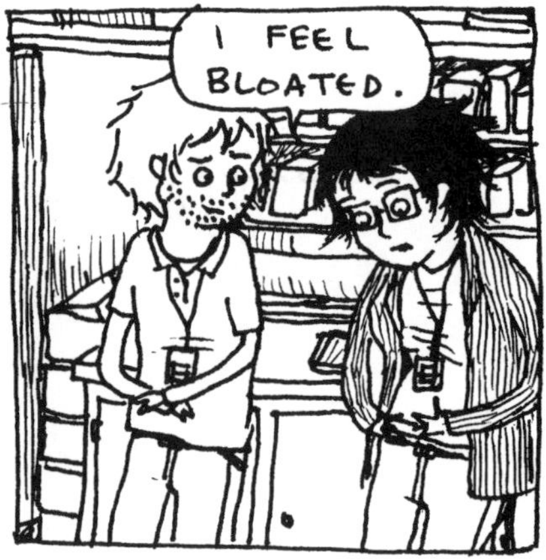
I FEEL BLOATED.

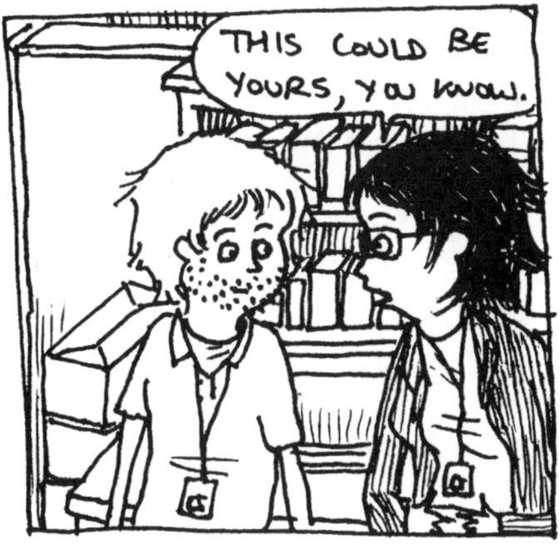
THIS COULD BE YOURS, YOU KNOW.

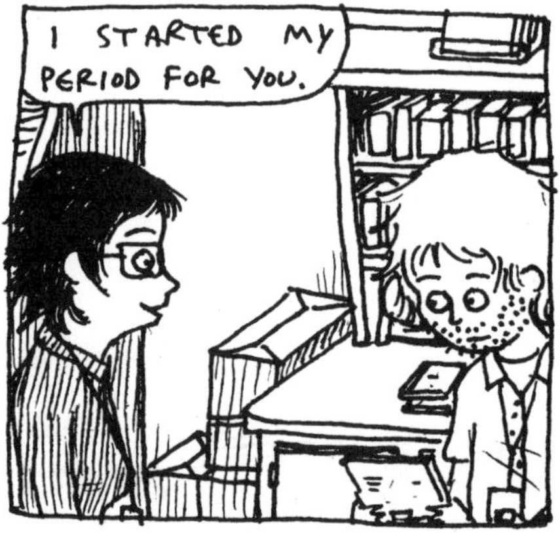
I STARTED MY PERIOD FOR YOU.

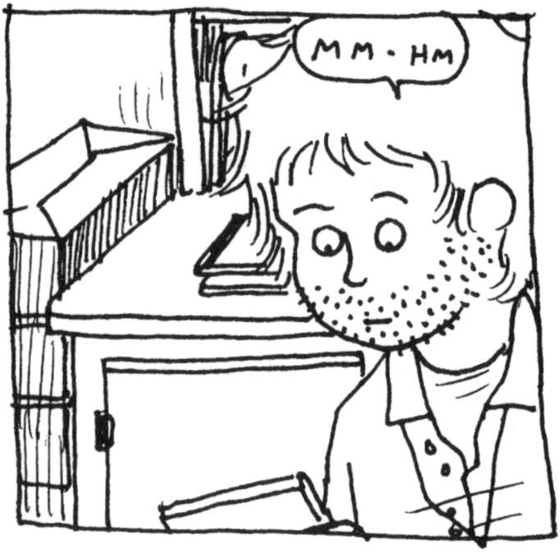
MM-HM

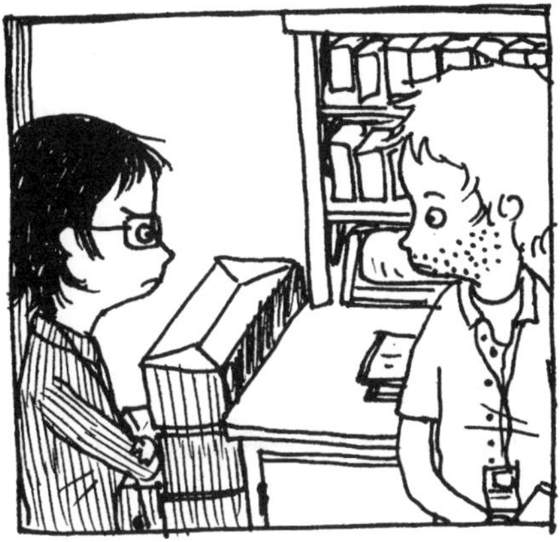

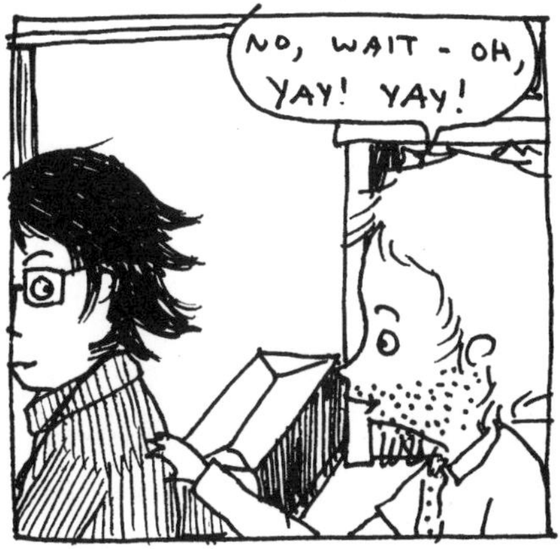
NO, WAIT - OH, YAY! YAY!

I WISH YOU DIDN'T HAVE TO WORK. WE COULD STILL BE LYING IN BED...
ME TOO.
HONKKKKK!
SOPHIA - STOP! YIELD SIGN!
HUH?
YIELD

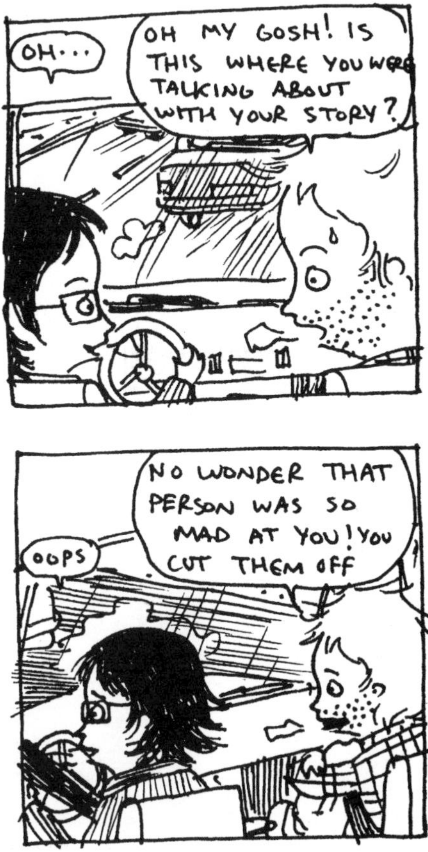
OH...
OH MY GOSH! IS THIS WHERE YOU WERE TALKING ABOUT WITH YOUR STORY?
OOPS
NO WONDER THAT PERSON WAS SO MAD AT YOU! YOU CUT THEM OFF

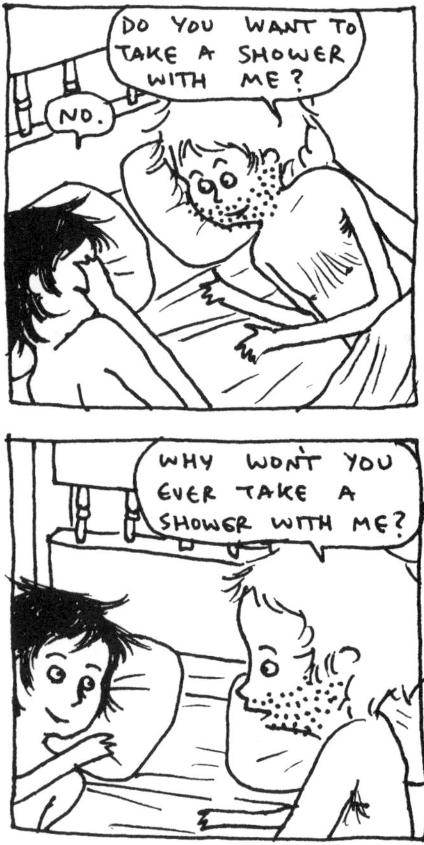
DO YOU WANT TO TAKE A SHOWER WITH ME?
NO.
WHY WON'T YOU EVER TAKE A SHOWER WITH ME?

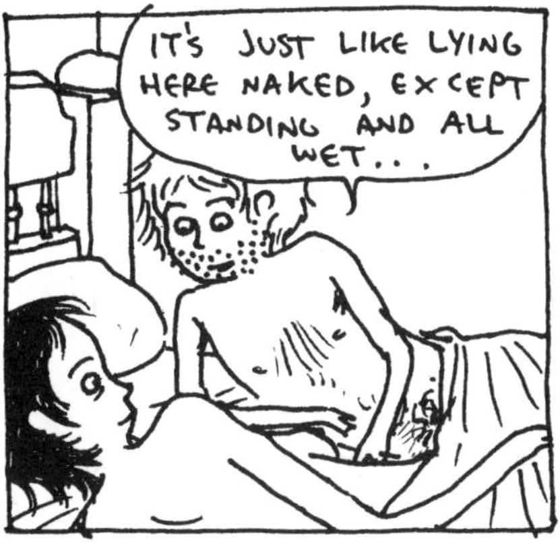
IT'S JUST LIKE LYING HERE NAKED, EXCEPT STANDING AND ALL WET...

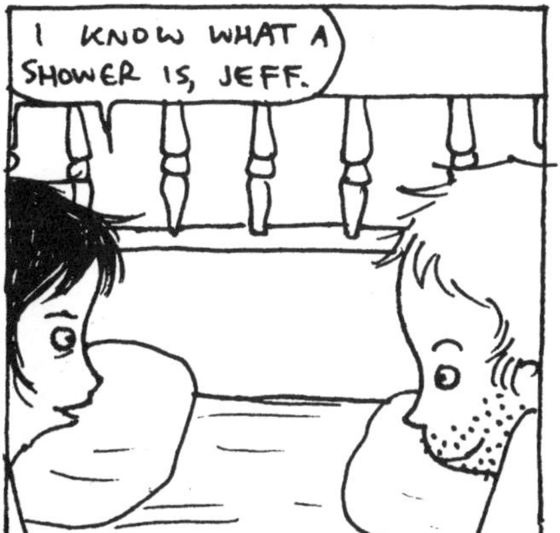
I KNOW WHAT A SHOWER IS, JEFF.

MY MOM REALLY LIKES YOU.
YEAH?

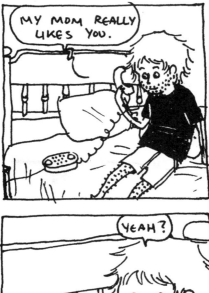

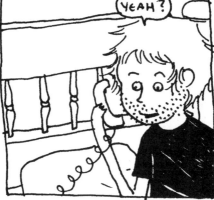

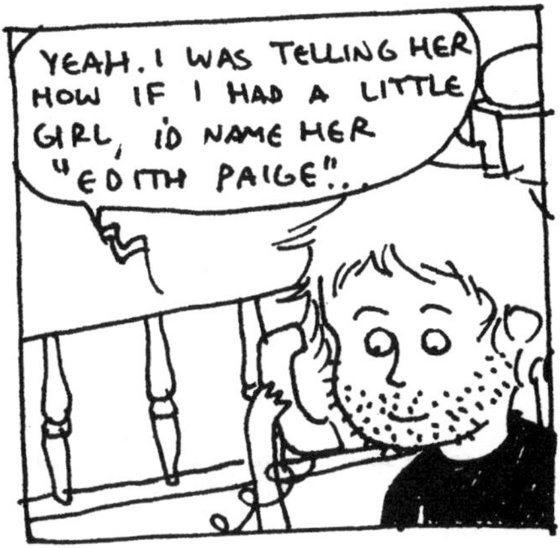
YEAH. I WAS TELLING HER HOW IF I HAD A LITTLE GIRL, I'D NAME HER "EDITH PAIGE"..

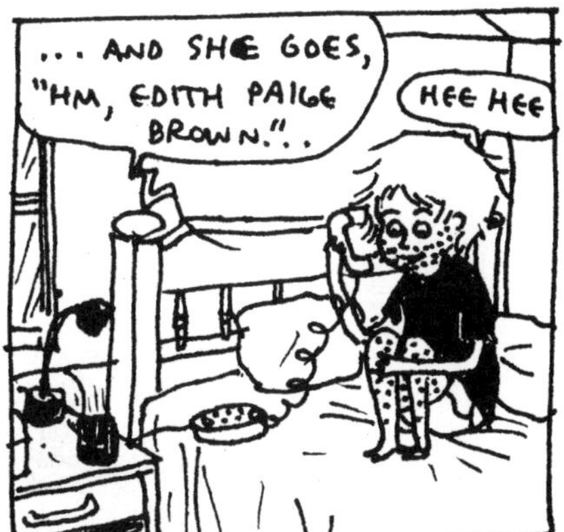
... AND SHE GOES, "HM, EDITH PAIGE BROWN."..
HEE HEE

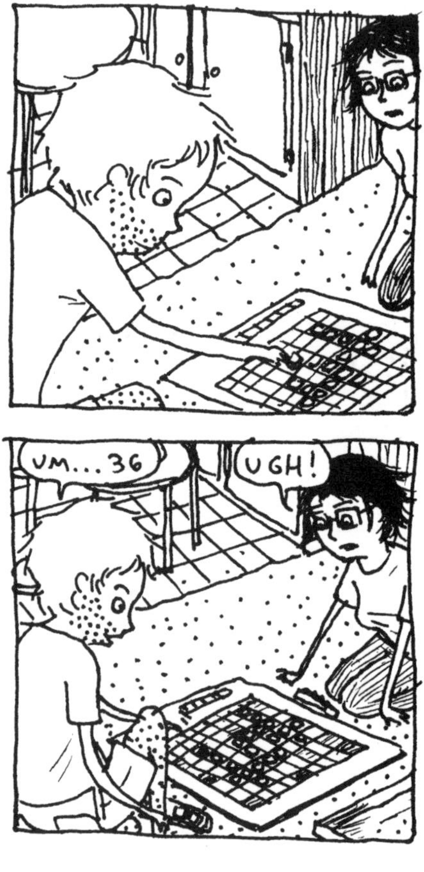
UM... 36
UGH!

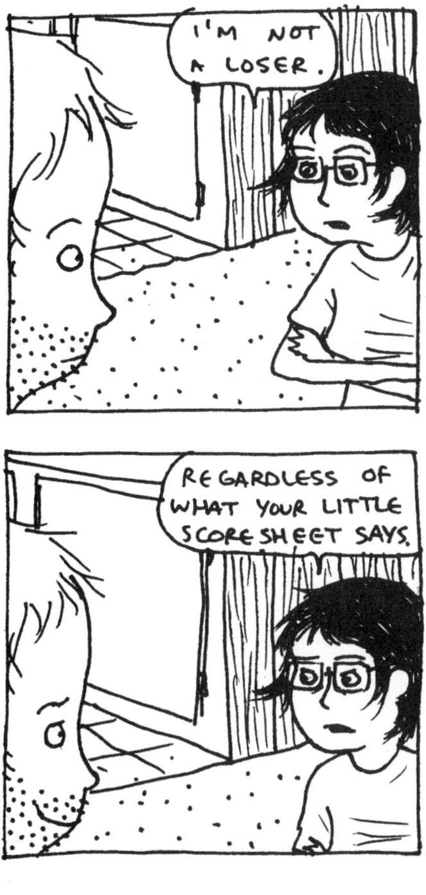
I'M NOT A LOSER.
REGARDLESS OF WHAT YOUR LITTLE SCORESHEET SAYS.

NOTES TO A FURTHER EXCUSE

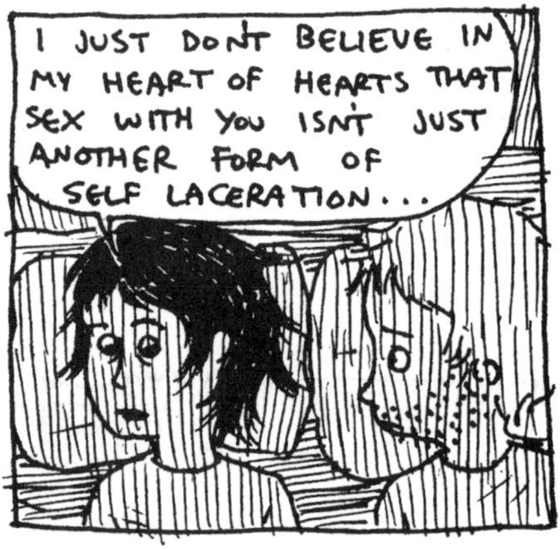
I JUST DON'T BELIEVE IN MY HEART OF HEARTS THAT SEX WITH YOU ISN'T JUST ANOTHER FORM OF SELF LACERATION...

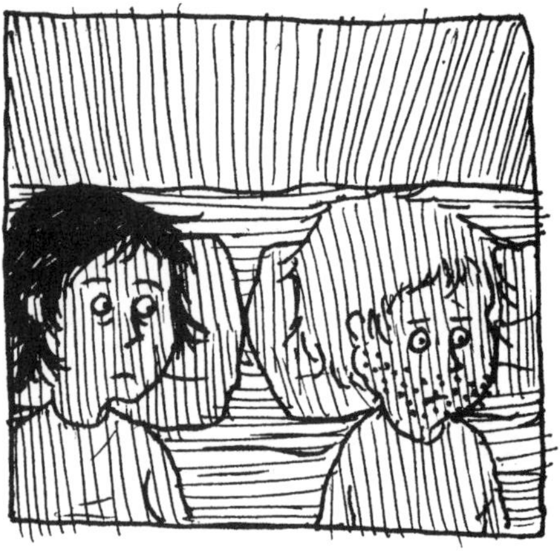

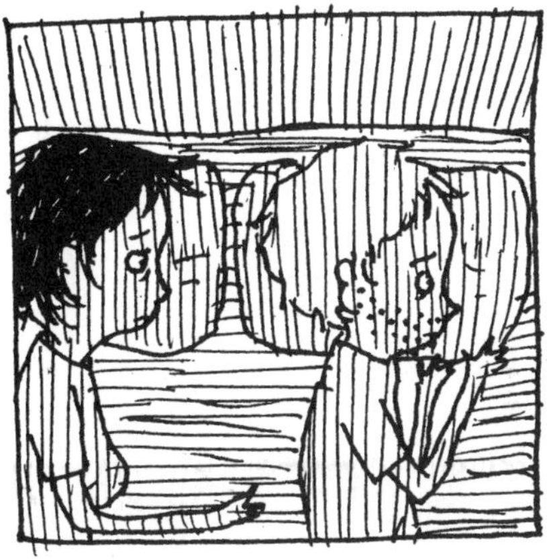

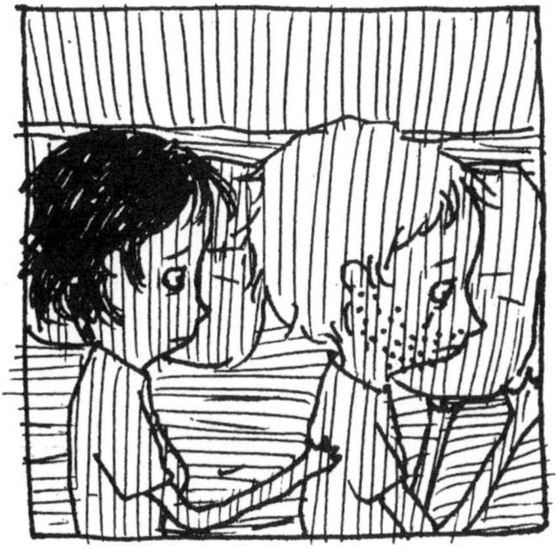

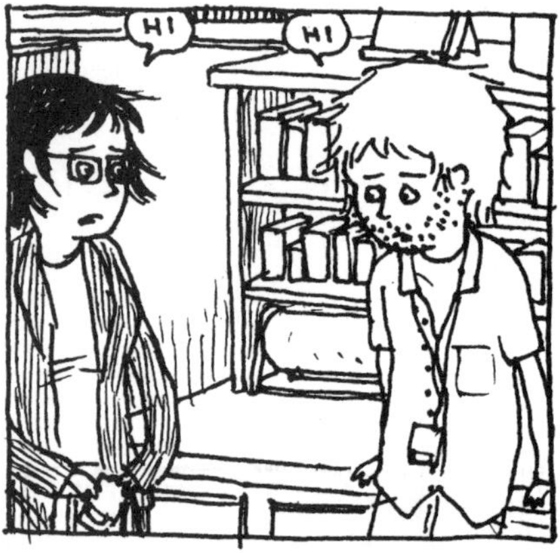
HI
HI

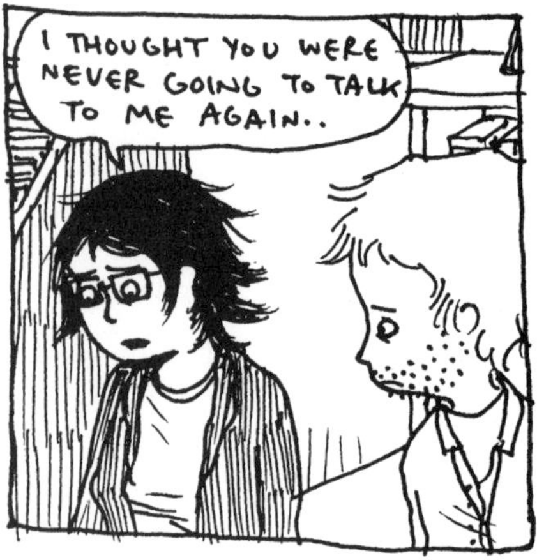
I THOUGHT YOU WERE NEVER GOING TO TALK TO ME AGAIN..

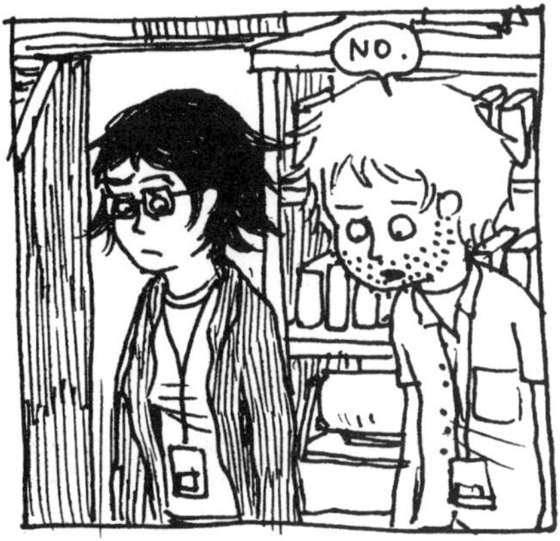
NO.

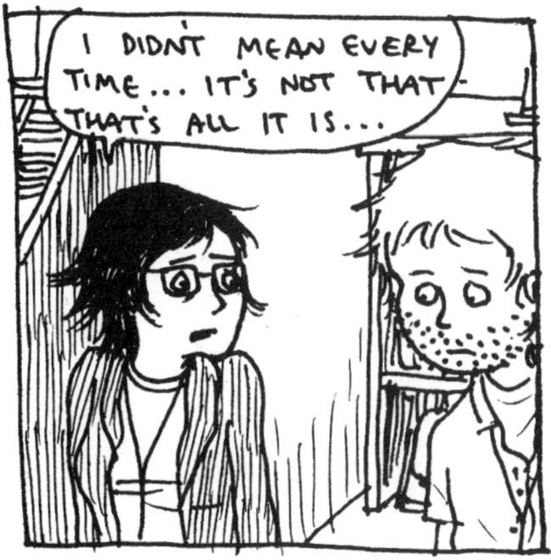
I DIDN'T MEAN EVERY TIME... IT'S NOT THAT THAT'S ALL IT IS...

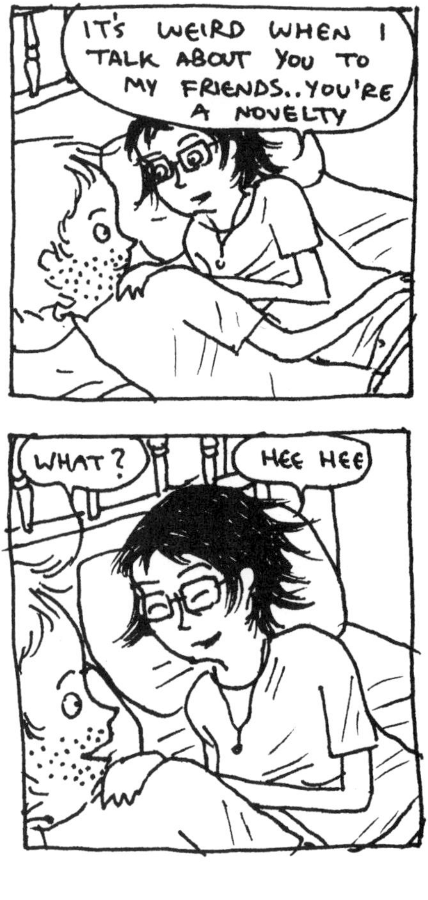
IT'S WEIRD WHEN I TALK ABOUT YOU TO MY FRIENDS..YOU'RE A NOVELTY
WHAT?
HEE HEE

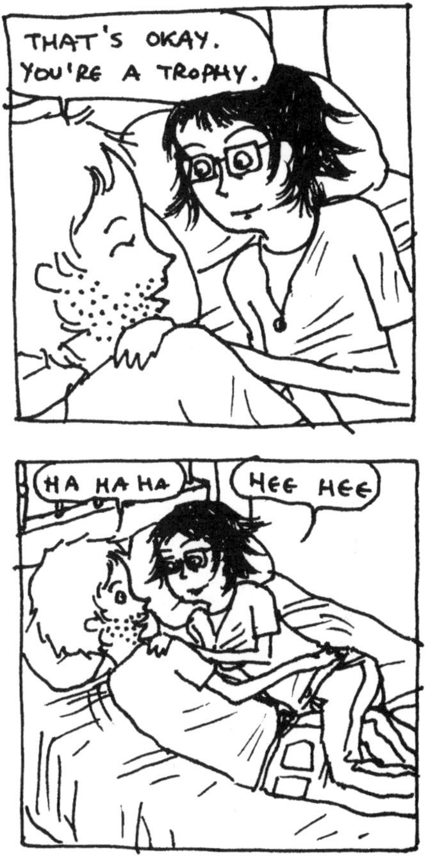
THAT'S OKAY. YOU'RE A TROPHY.
HA HA HA
HEE HEE

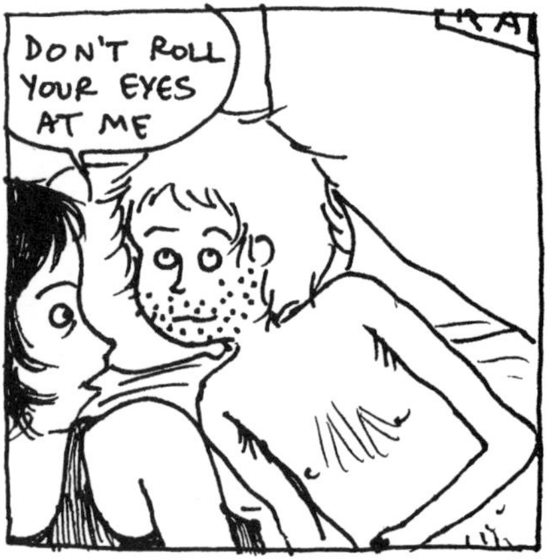
DON'T ROLL YOUR EYES AT ME

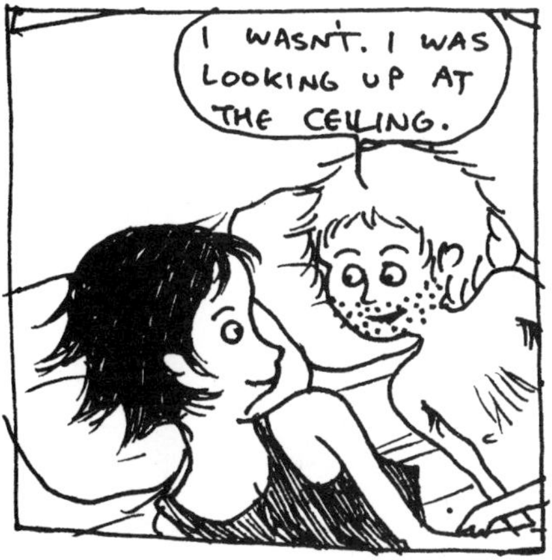
I WASN'T. I WAS LOOKING UP AT THE CEILING.

ANYBODY CAN DRAW

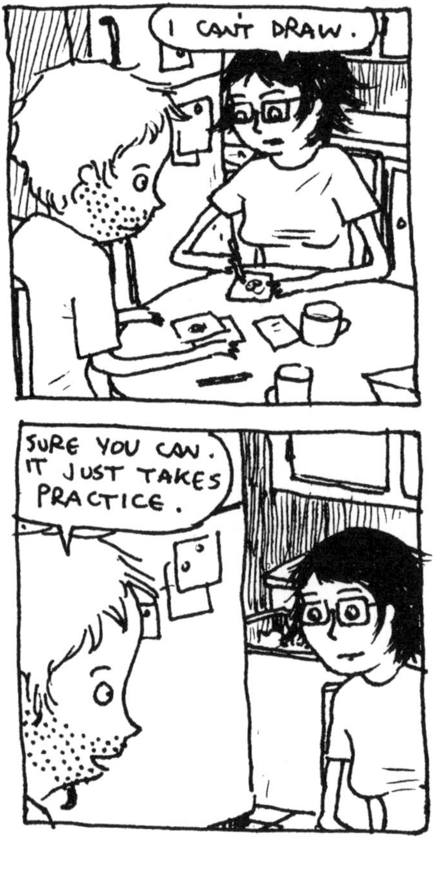
I CAN'T DRAW.
SURE YOU CAN. IT JUST TAKES PRACTICE.

SEE? NOW LOOK AT THE ANGLE OF THAT LINE...

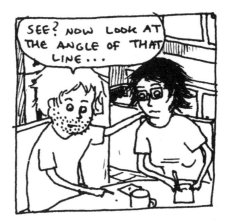

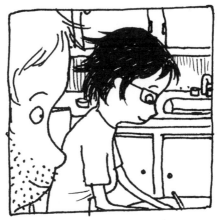

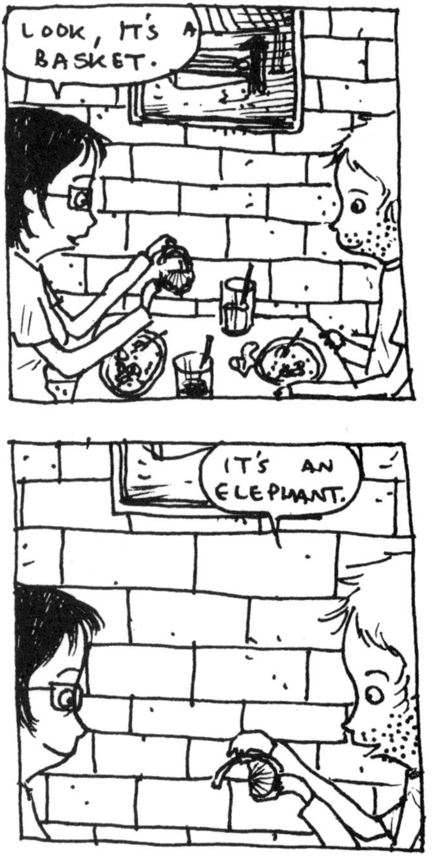
LOOK, IT'S A BASKET.
IT'S AN ELEPHANT.

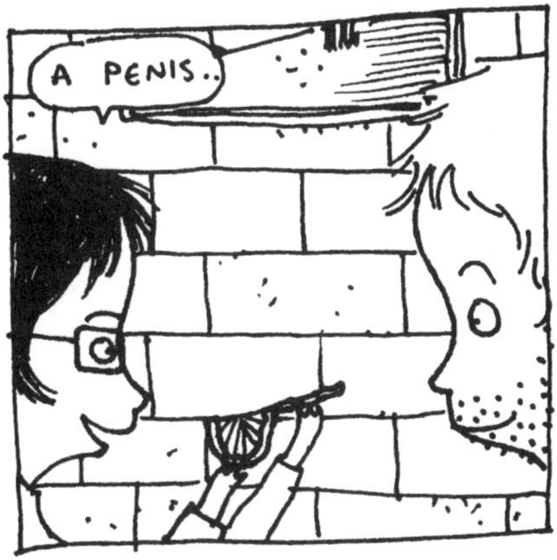
A PENIS..

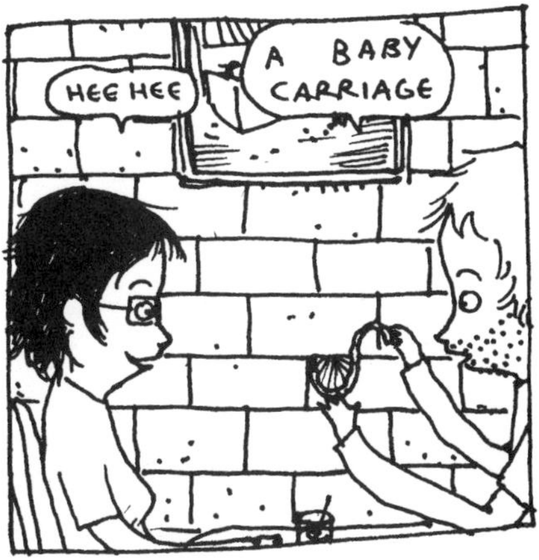
A BABY CARRIAGE
HEE HEE

LOOK.
IT'S KIND OF PHALLIC
OH MY GOSH! LOOK AT THE PEW!

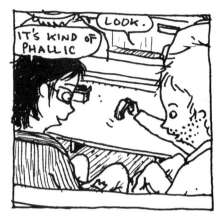

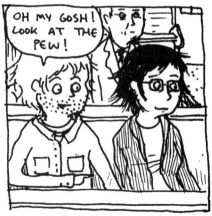

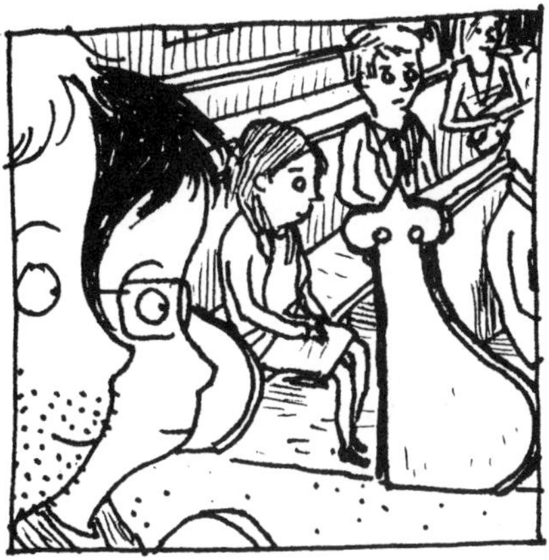

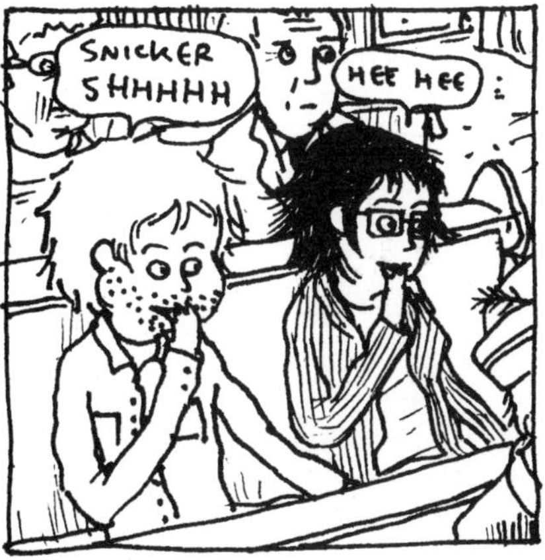
SNICKER
SHHHHH
HEE HEE

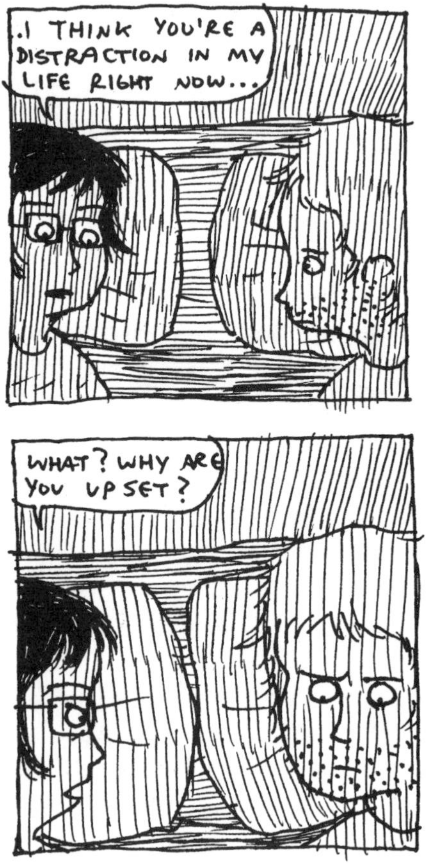
.I THINK YOU'RE A DISTRACTION IN MY LIFE RIGHT NOW...
WHAT? WHY ARE YOU UPSET?

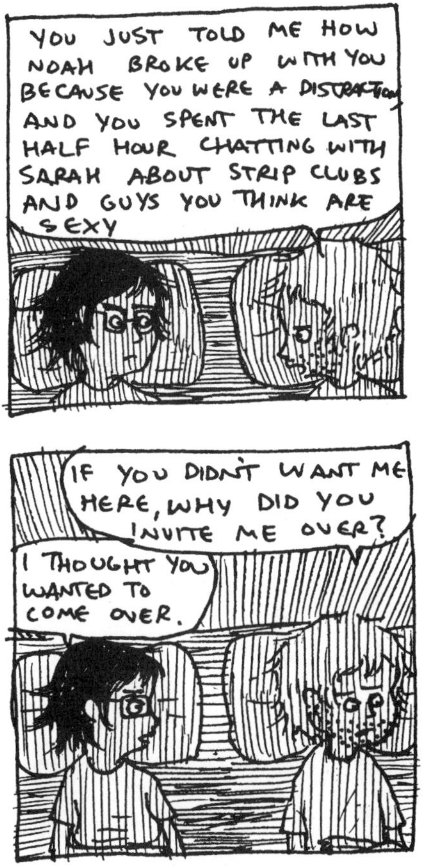
YOU JUST TOLD ME HOW NOAH BROKE UP WITH YOU BECAUSE YOU WERE A DISTRACTION AND YOU SPENT THE LAST HALF HOUR CHATTING WITH SARAH ABOUT STRIP CLUBS AND GUYS YOU THINK ARE SEXY
IF YOU DIDN'T WANT ME HERE, WHY DID YOU INVITE ME OVER?
I THOUGHT YOU WANTED TO COME OVER.

THE SOUND OF FADING SHADOWS

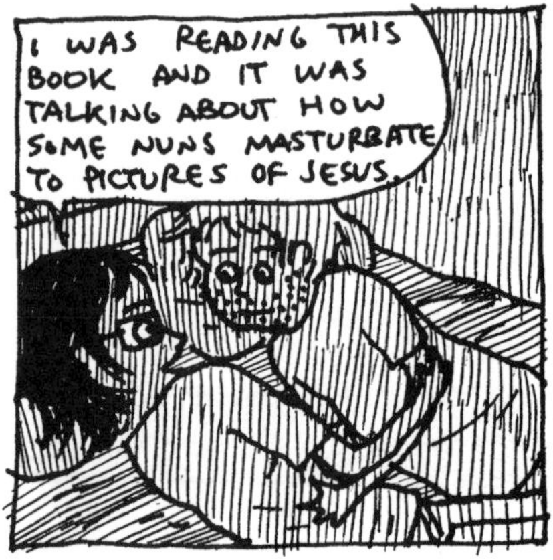
I WAS READING THIS BOOK AND IT WAS TALKING ABOUT HOW SOME NUNS MASTURBATE TO PICTURES OF JESUS.

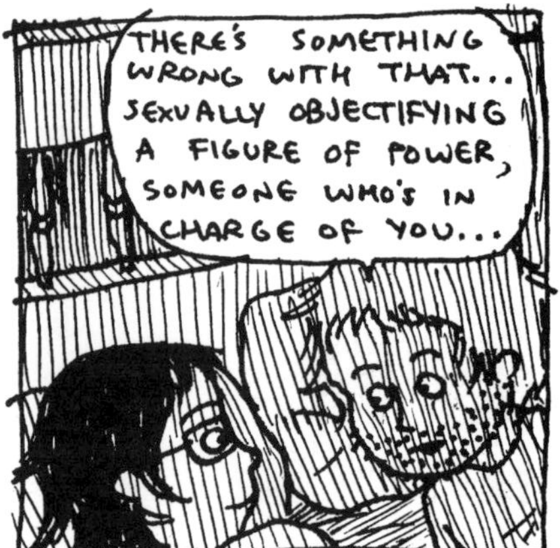
THERE'S SOMETHING WRONG WITH THAT... SEXUALLY OBJECTIFYING A FIGURE OF POWER, SOMEONE WHO'S IN CHARGE OF YOU...

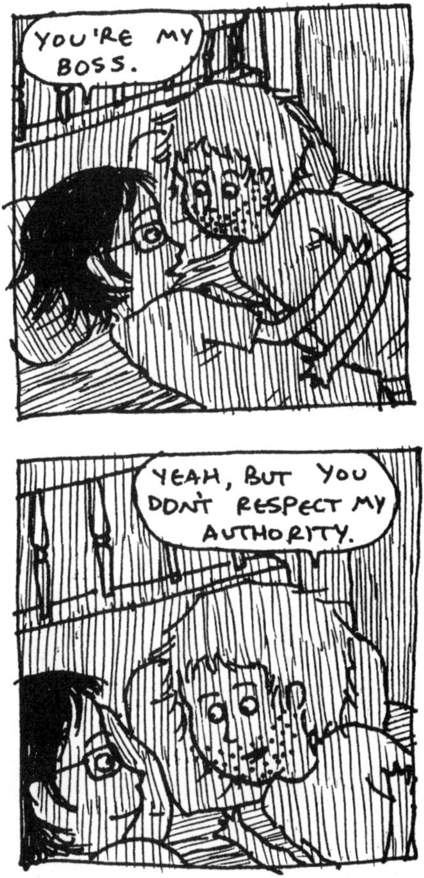
YOU'RE MY BOSS.
YEAH, BUT YOU DON'T RESPECT MY AUTHORITY.

DO YOU WANT TO HEAR MY TRAIN IMPRESSION AGAIN?
NO.
EEEEEEEEEEEEEE

YES IT IS. IT'S THE TRAIN STOPPING.
THAT'S NOT EVEN CLOSE.
WOOOOOOOOOHH
HA HA HA!

DID YOU

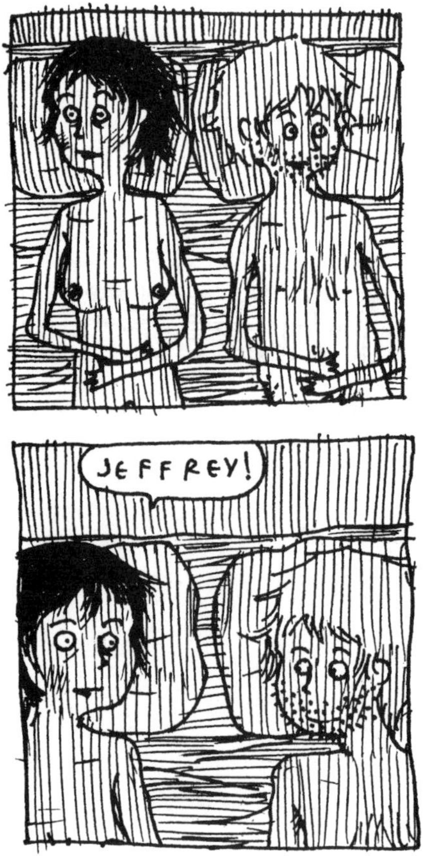
JEFFREY!

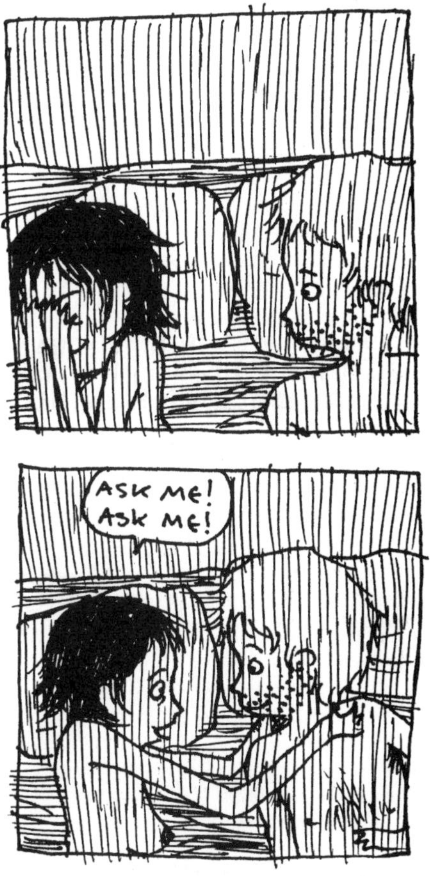
ASK ME!
ASK ME!

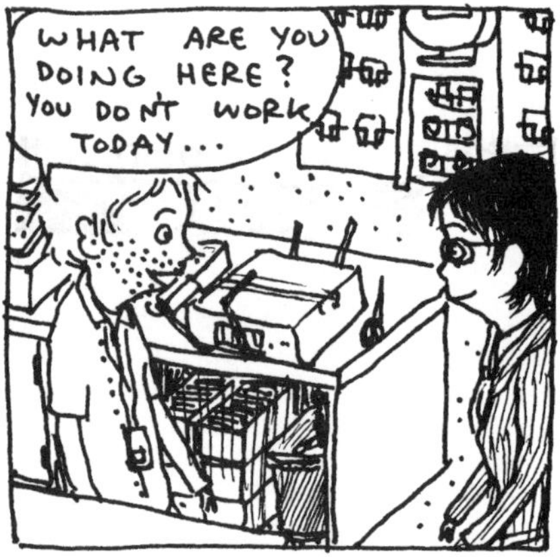
WHAT ARE YOU DOING HERE? YOU DON'T WORK TODAY...

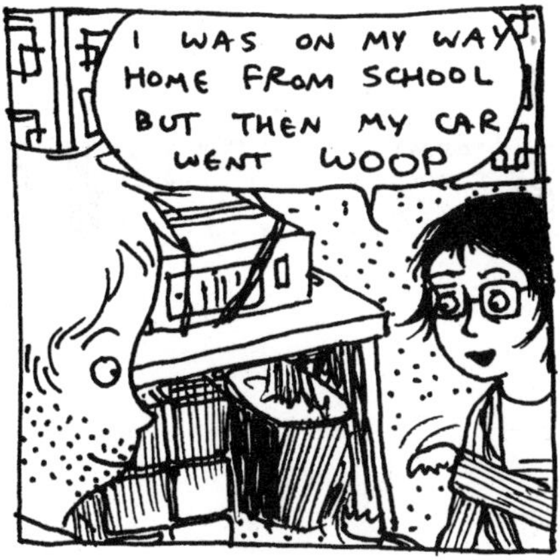
I WAS ON MY WAY HOME FROM SCHOOL BUT THEN MY CAR WENT WOOP

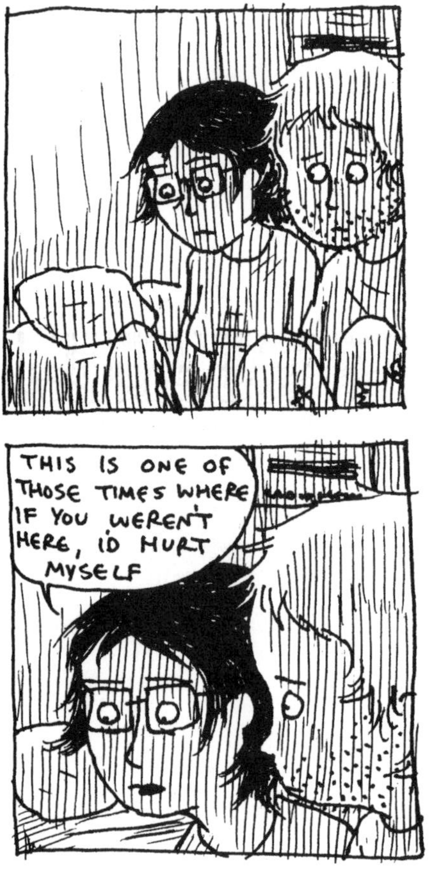
THIS IS ONE OF THOSE TIMES WHERE IF YOU WEREN'T HERE, ID HURT MYSELF

MARCH

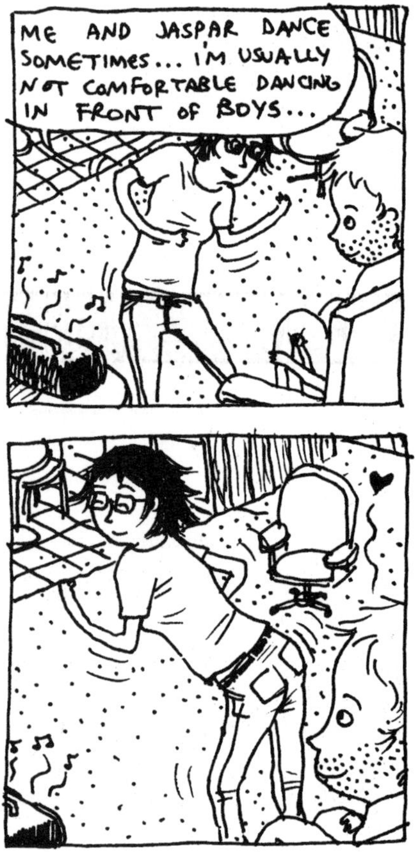
ME AND JASPAR DANCE SOMETIMES... I'M USUALLY NOT COMFORTABLE DANCING IN FRONT OF BOYS...

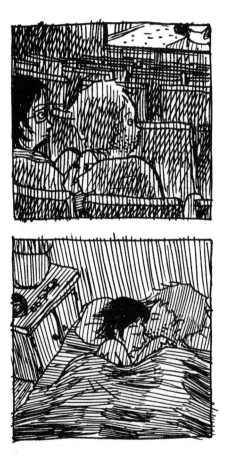

RUB TO AGITATE

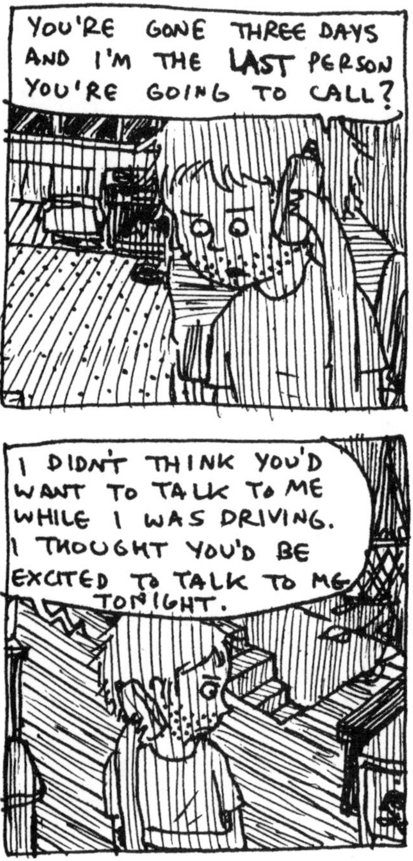
YOU'RE GONE THREE DAYS AND I'M THE LAST PERSON YOU'RE GOING TO CALL?
I DIDN'T THINK YOU'D WANT TO TALK TO ME WHILE I WAS DRIVING. I THOUGHT YOU'D BE EXCITED TO TALK TO ME TONIGHT.

YEAH, AND I LEFT MESSAGES. DIDN'T YOU GET THEM? YOU COULDN'T AT LEAST CALL AND SAY WHEN YOU'D BE HOME?

OH MY GOD. I CAN'T BELIEVE YOU'RE THIS ANGRY!

YOU KNOW, MAYBE YOU DON'T WANT TO BE IN A ROMANTIC RELATIONSHIP WITH ME.
MAYBE I DON'T WANT TO BE IN A ROMANTIC RELATIONSHIP WITH SOMEONE WHO CHECKS UP ON ME EVERY TWO HOURS, WHO I CAN'T GO ONE DAY WITHOUT CALLING

I DON'T WANT TO DO THIS.
FINE.

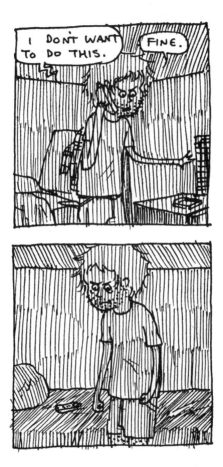

BROKEN

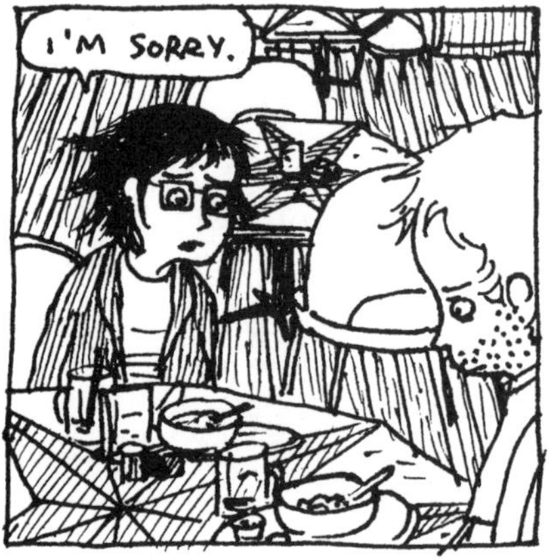
I'M SORRY.

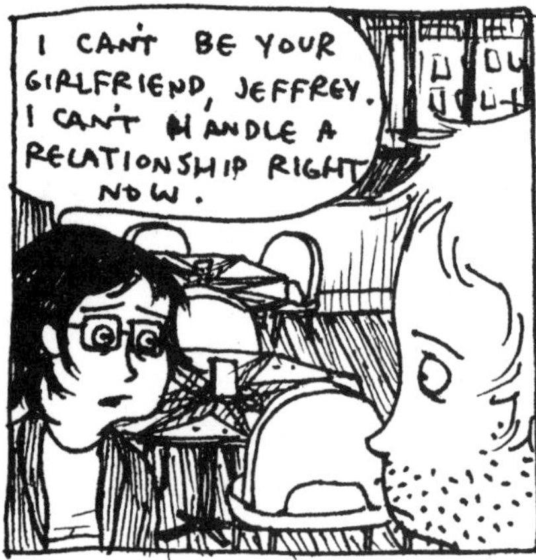
I CAN'T BE YOUR GIRLFRIEND, JEFFREY. I CAN'T HANDLE A RELATIONSHIP RIGHT NOW.

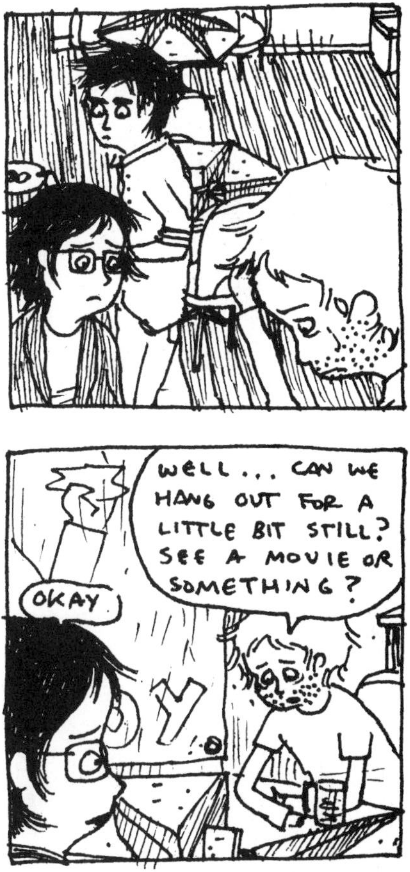
WELL... CAN WE HANG OUT FOR A LITTLE BIT STILL? SEE A MOVIE OR SOMETHING?
OKAY

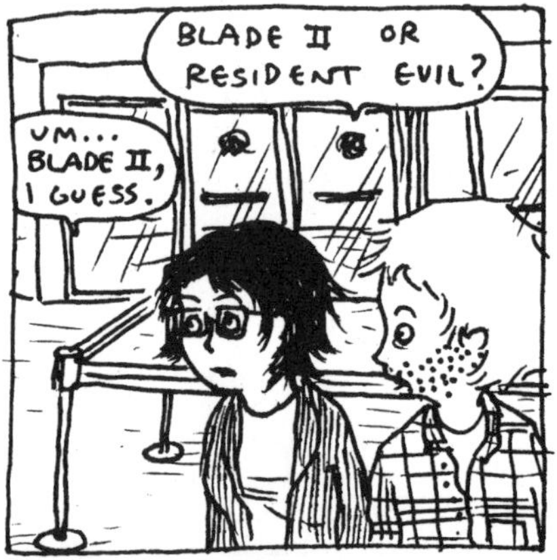
BLADE II OR RESIDENT EVIL?
UM... BLADE II, I GUESS.

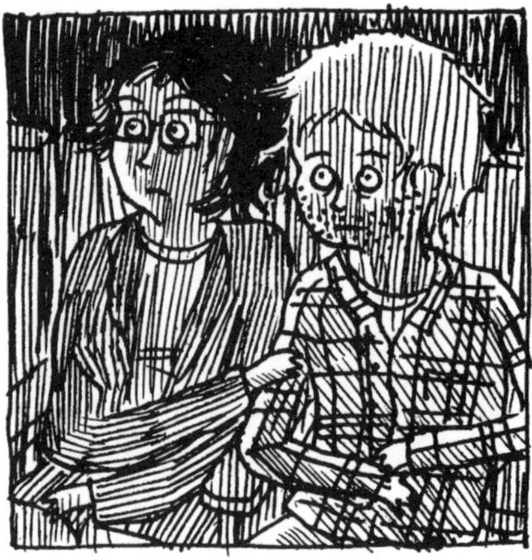

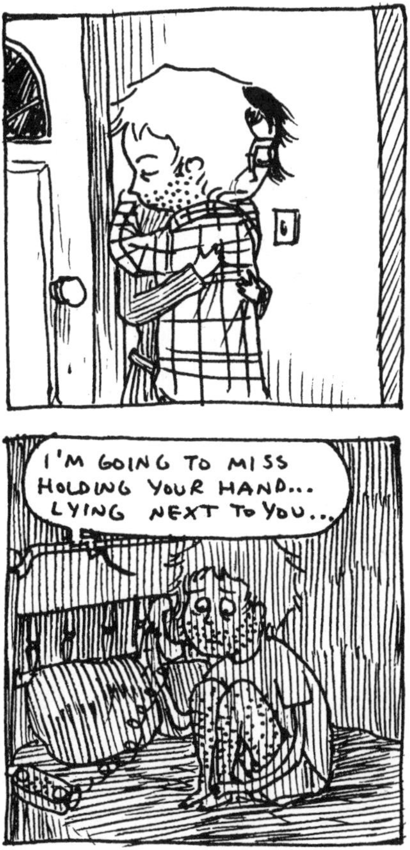
I'M GOING TO MISS HOLDING YOUR HAND... LYING NEXT TO YOU...

CARLOS'

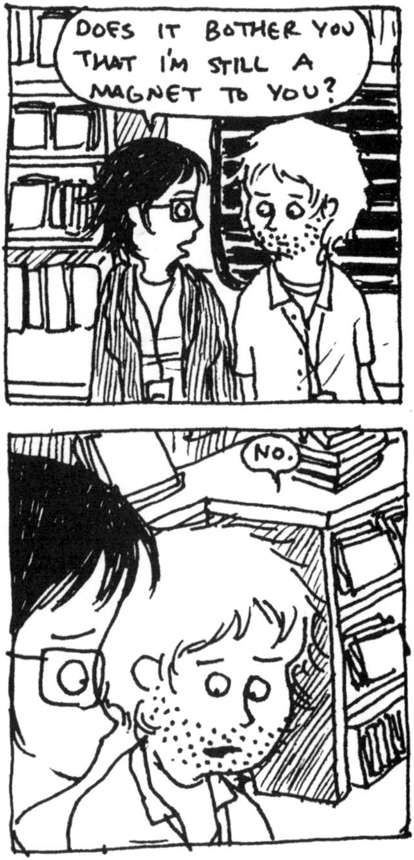
DOES IT BOTHER YOU THAT I'M STILL A MAGNET TO YOU?
NO.

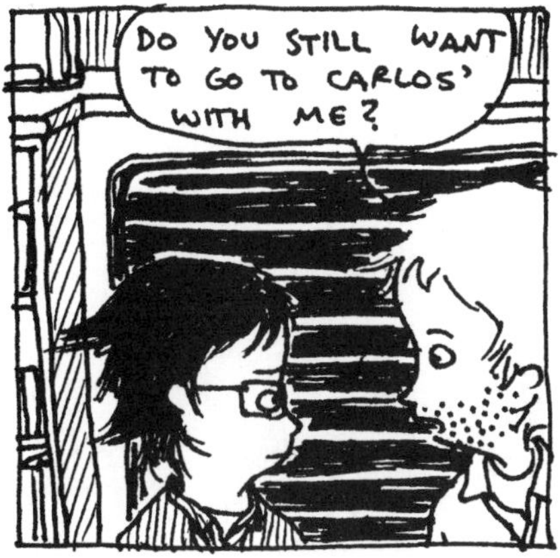
DO YOU STILL WANT TO GO TO CARLOS' WITH ME?

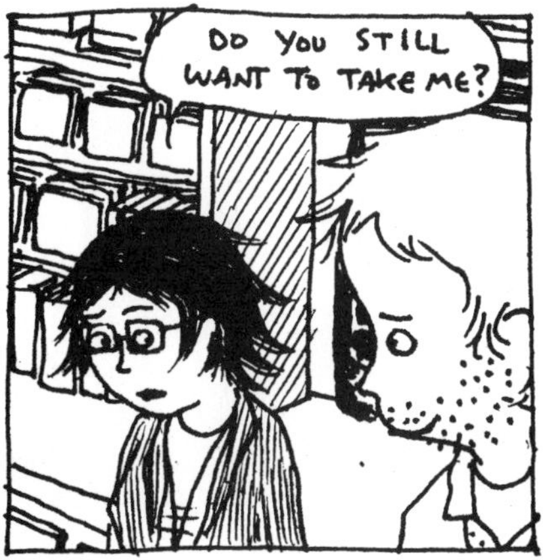
DO YOU STILL WANT TO TAKE ME?

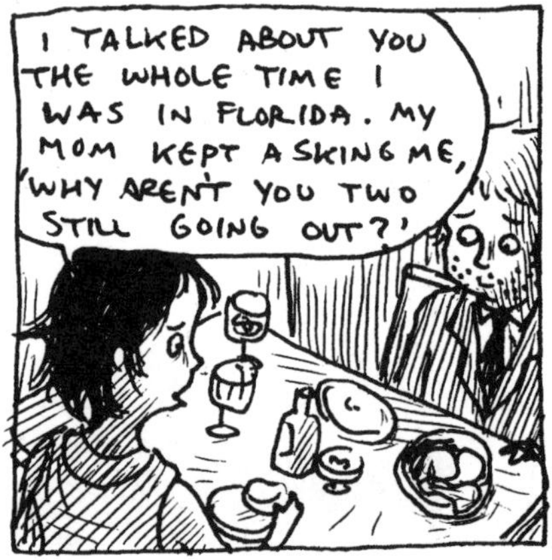
I TALKED ABOUT YOU THE WHOLE TIME I WAS IN FLORIDA. MY MOM KEPT ASKING ME, 'WHY AREN'T YOU TWO STILL GOING OUT?'

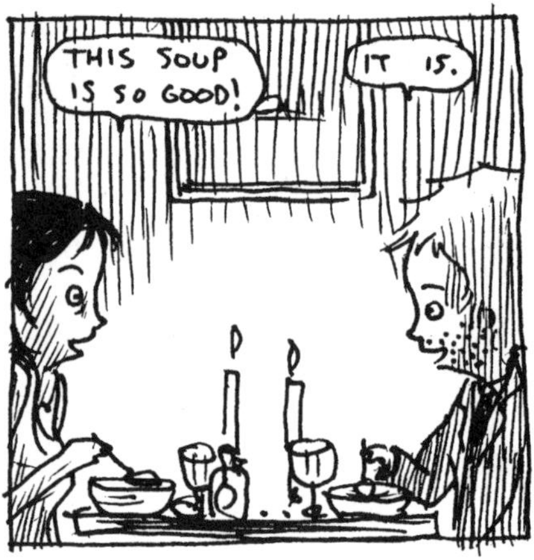
THIS SOUP IS SO GOOD!
IT IS.

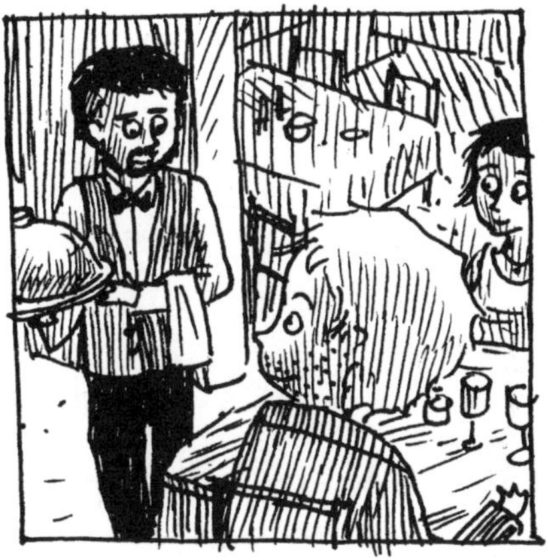

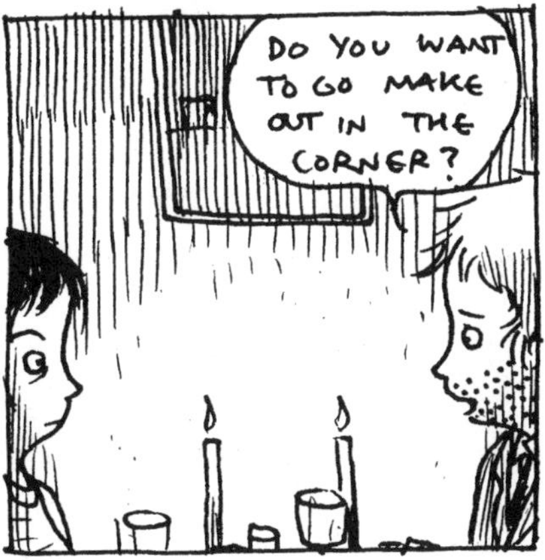
DO YOU WANT TO GO MAKE OUT IN THE CORNER?

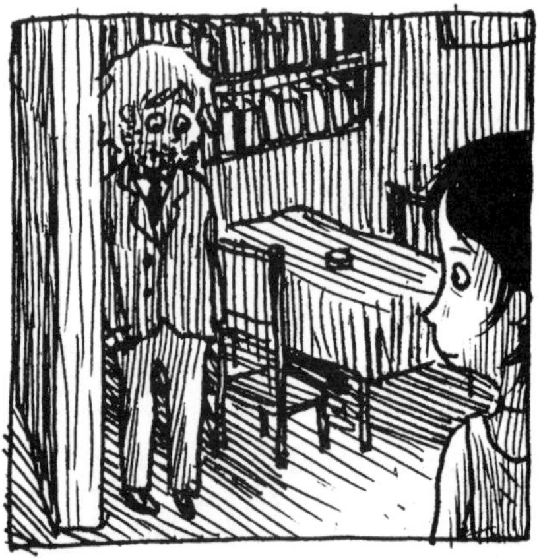
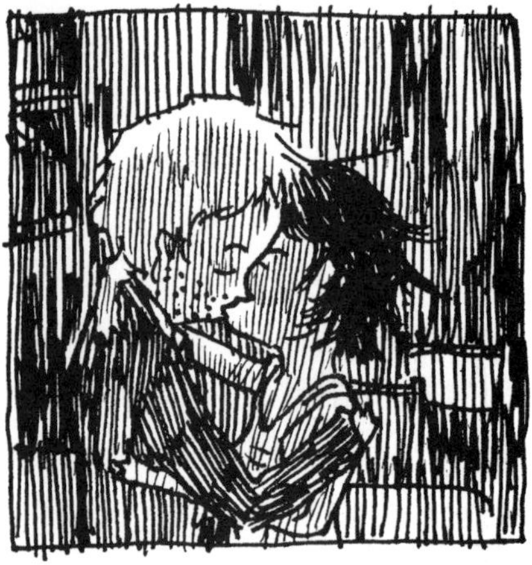

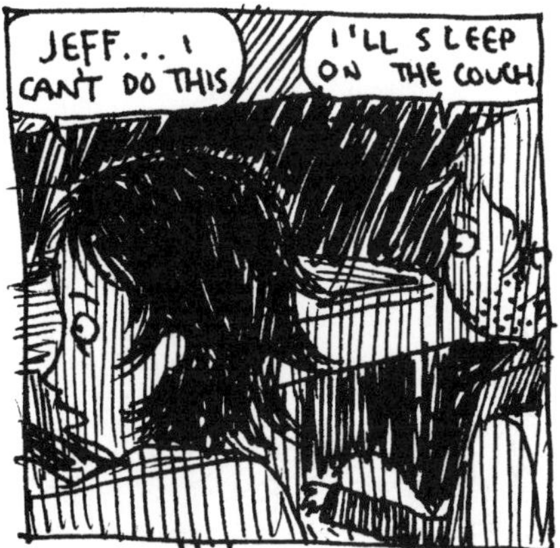
JEFF... I CAN'T DO THIS
I'LL SLEEP ON THE COUCH

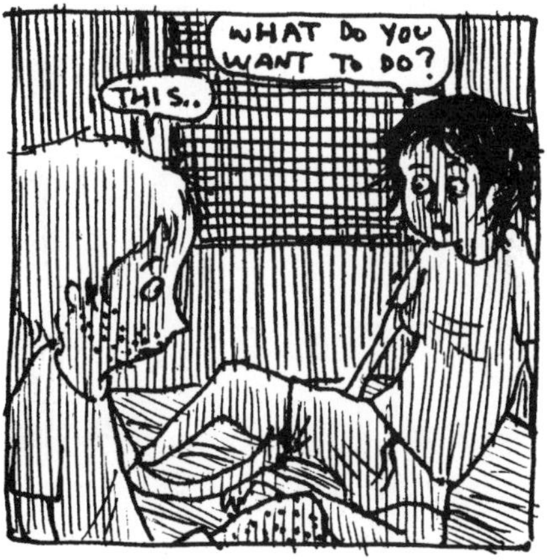
WHAT DO YOU WANT TO DO?
THIS..

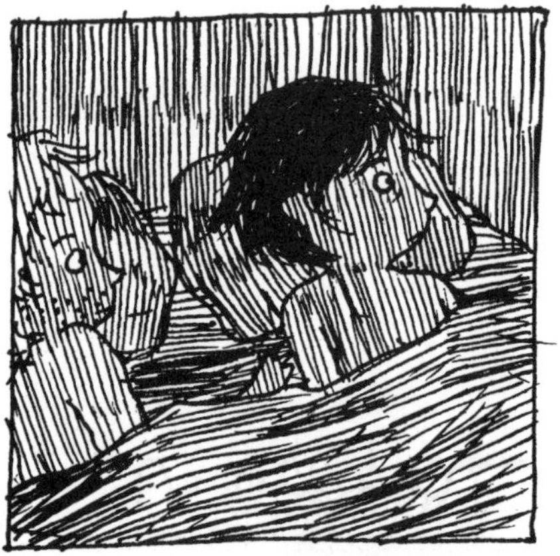

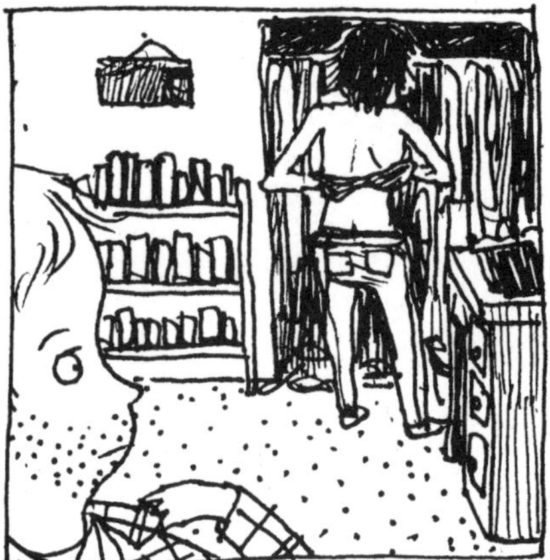

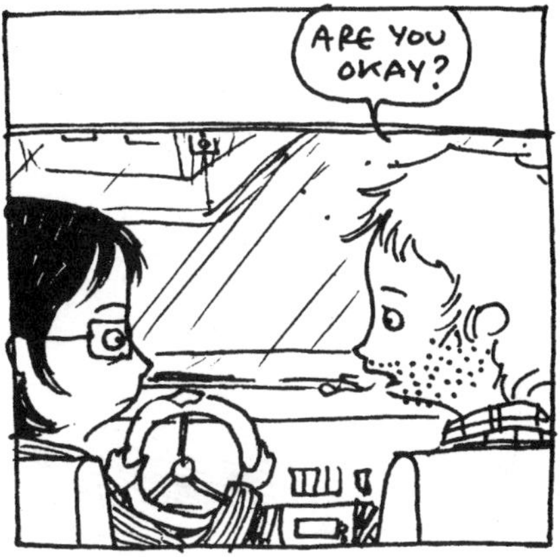
ARE YOU OKAY?

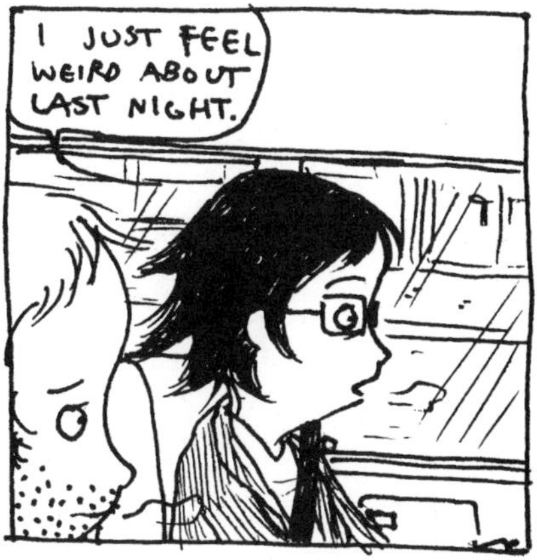
I JUST FEEL WEIRD ABOUT LAST NIGHT.

A DIFFERENT PLACE THEN

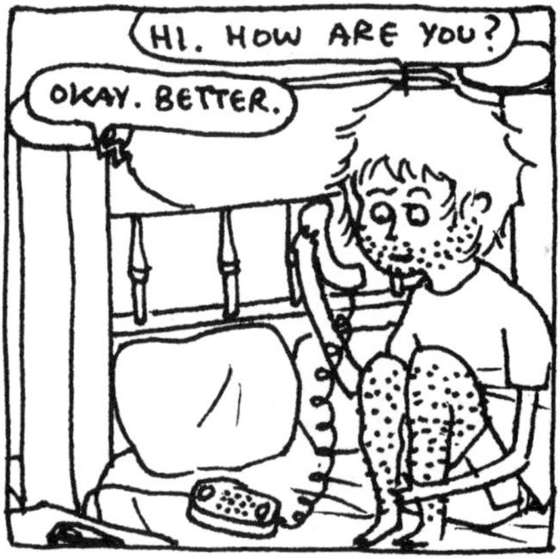
HI. HOW ARE YOU?
OKAY. BETTER.

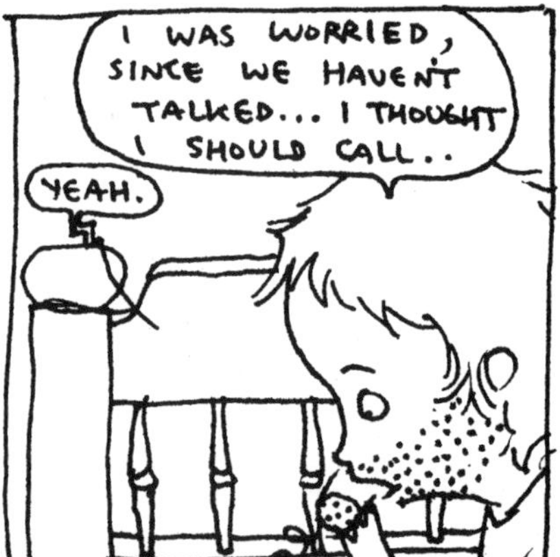
I WAS WORRIED, SINCE WE HAVEN'T TALKED... I THOUGHT I SHOULD CALL..
YEAH.

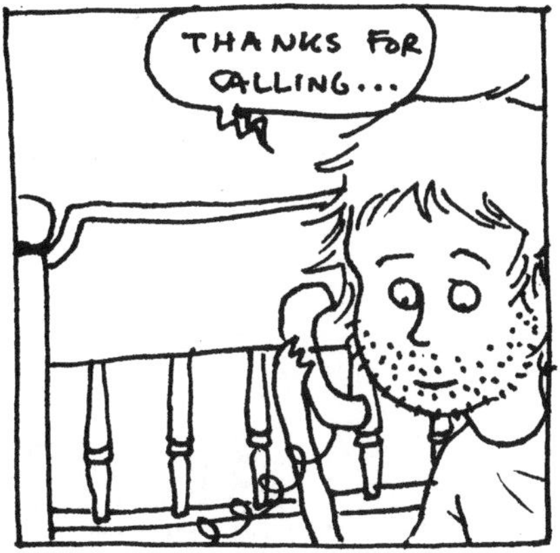
THANKS FOR CALLING...

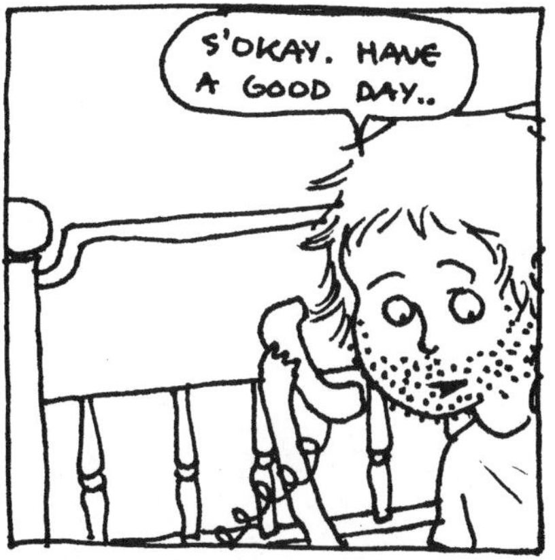
S'OKAY. HAVE A GOOD DAY..

THE NIGHT AFTER THE MORNING AFTER

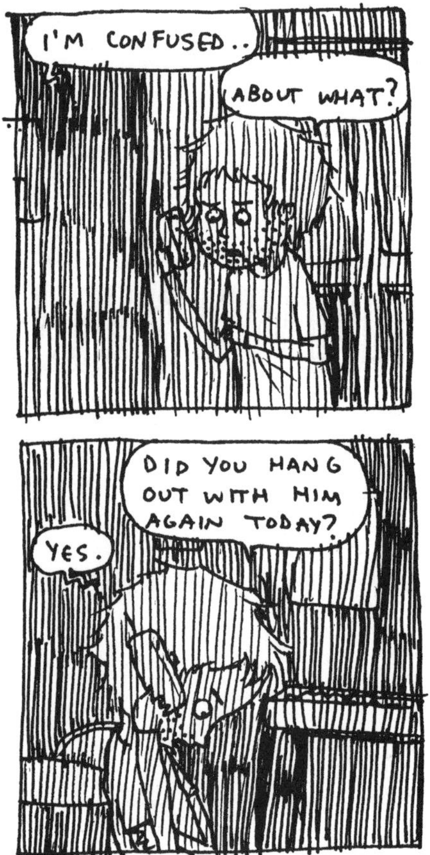
I'M CONFUSED..
ABOUT WHAT?
DID YOU HANG OUT WITH HIM AGAIN TODAY?
YES.

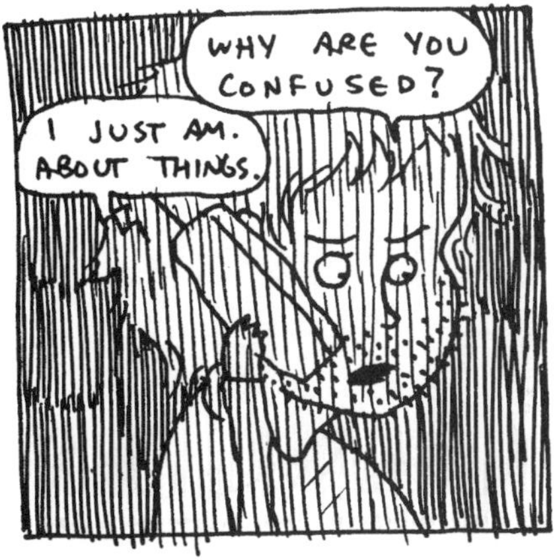
WHY ARE YOU CONFUSED?
I JUST AM. ABOUT THINGS.

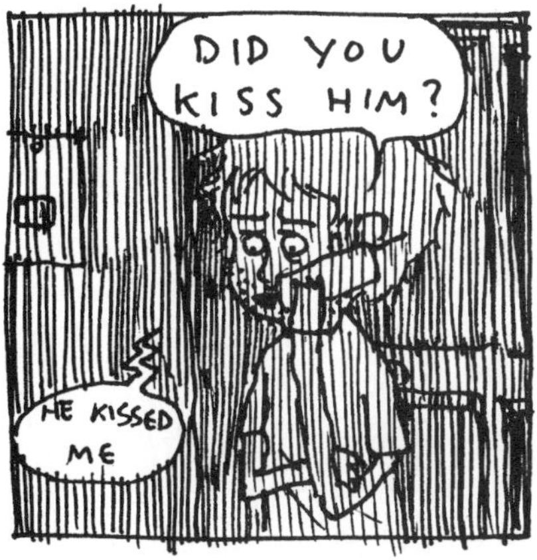
DID YOU KISS HIM?
HE KISSED ME

FUCK

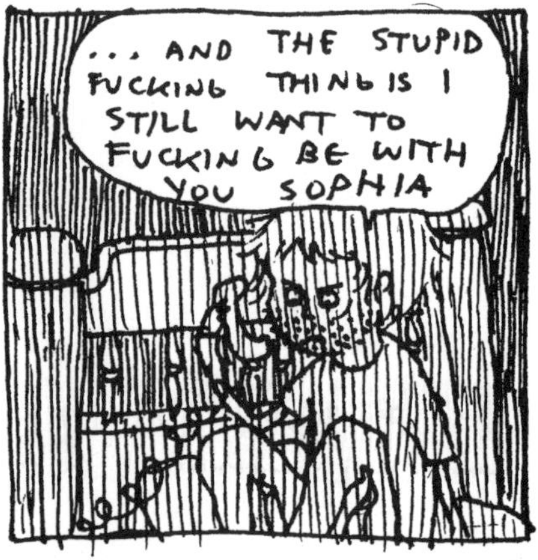

... AND THE STUPID FUCKING THING IS I STILL WANT TO FUCKING BE WITH YOU SOPHIA

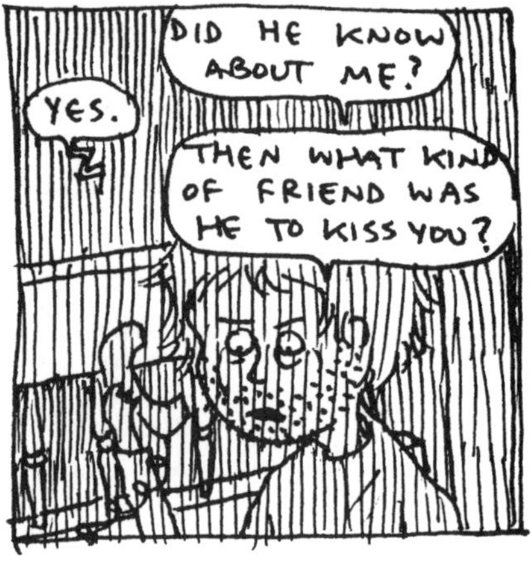

DID HE KNOW ABOUT ME?
YES.
THEN WHAT KIND OF FRIEND WAS HE TO KISS YOU?

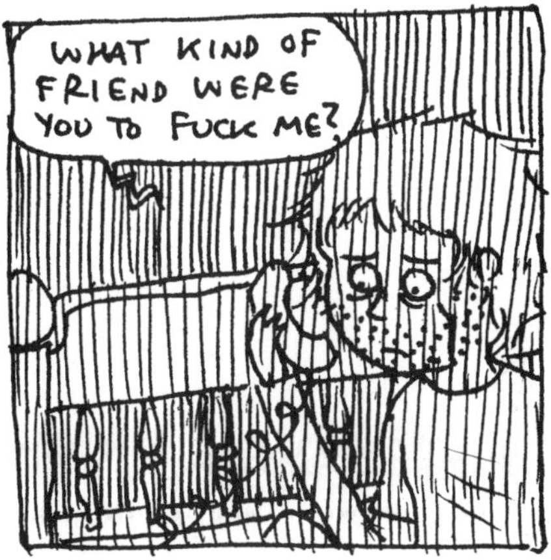
WHAT KIND OF FRIEND WERE YOU TO FUCK ME?

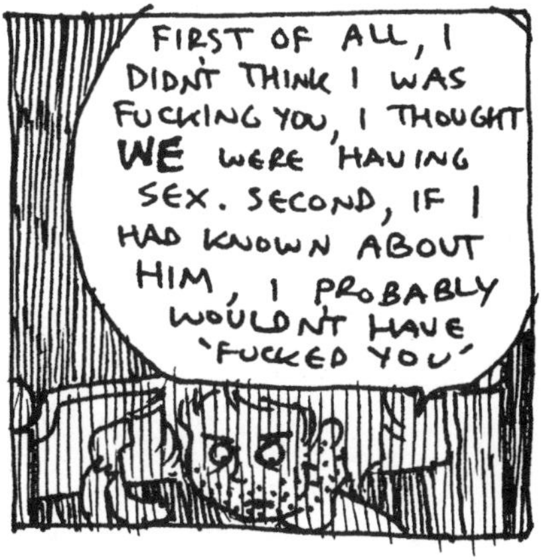
FIRST OF ALL, I DIDN'T THINK I WAS FUCKING YOU, I THOUGHT WE WERE HAVING SEX. SECOND, IF I HAD KNOWN ABOUT HIM, I PROBABLY WOULDN'T HAVE 'FUCKED YOU'

D A N I E L :

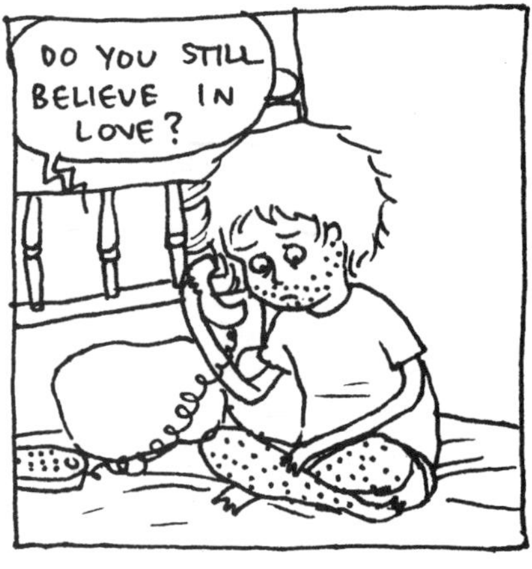
DO YOU STILL BELIEVE IN LOVE?

ME:

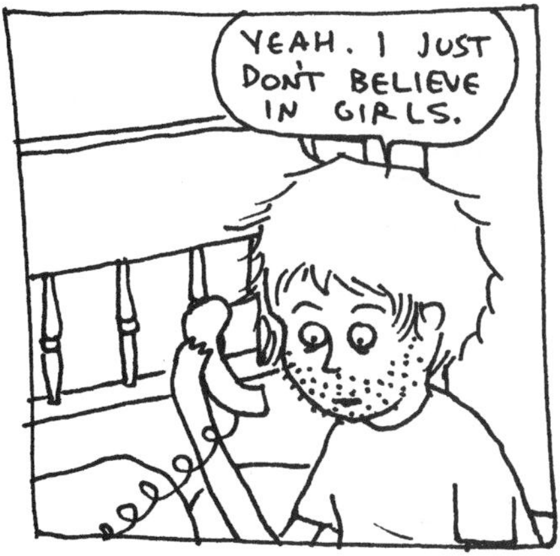
YEAH. I JUST DON'T BELIEVE IN GIRLS.

I DIDN'T CHEAT ON YOU. I'M NOT YOUR GIRLFRIEND, JEFF.
YEAH, BUT YOU LIED TO ME. YOU TOLD ME AGAIN AND AGAIN, THERE'S NO OTHER BOYS

I'M SORRY. WE CONNECTED... WE HAD SIMILAR EXPERIENCES IN OREGON... WHEN DID YOU EVER TALK TO ME ABOUT GOD OR RELIGION?
WE DID TALK ABOUT GOD! AND IF IT WAS SO IMPORTANT TO YOU, WHY DIDN'T YOU BRING IT UP EVER?

I'M SORRY I KISSED HIM. I'D TAKE THAT BACK IF I COULD. I THOUGHT ABOUT YOU THE WHOLE TIME I WAS WITH HIM..

I LIKE YOU, JEFFREY, BUT I STILL CAN'T BE YOUR GIRLFRIEND.
139

SOAKING WET

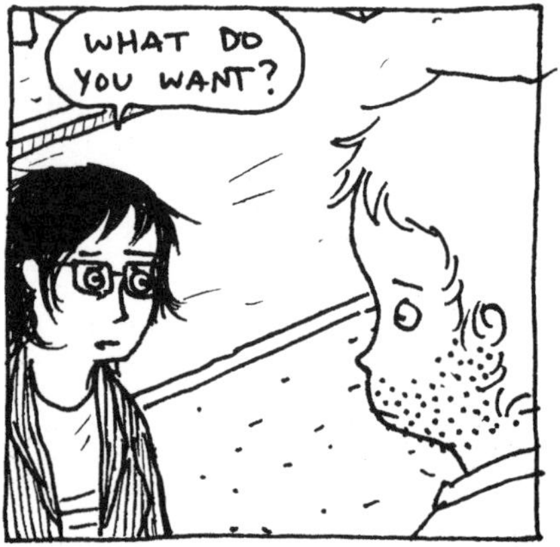
WHAT DO YOU WANT?

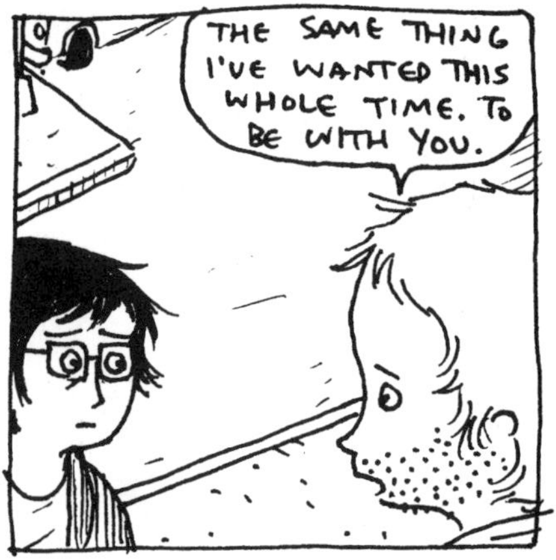
THE SAME THING I'VE WANTED THIS WHOLE TIME. TO BE WITH YOU.

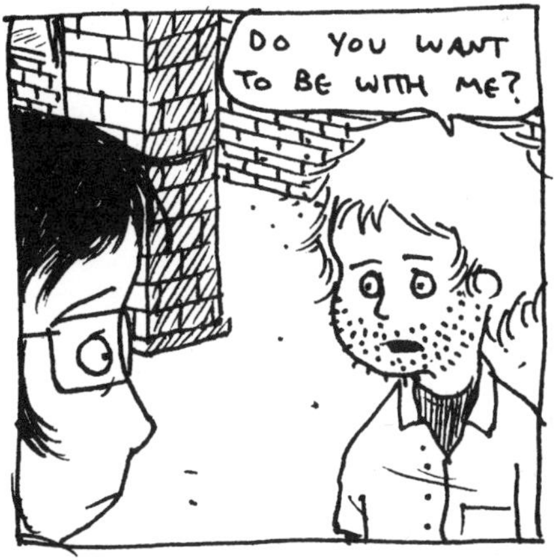
DO YOU WANT TO BE WITH ME?

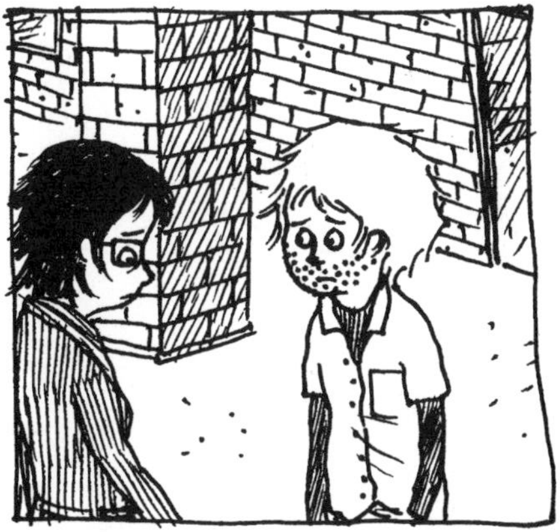

APRIL

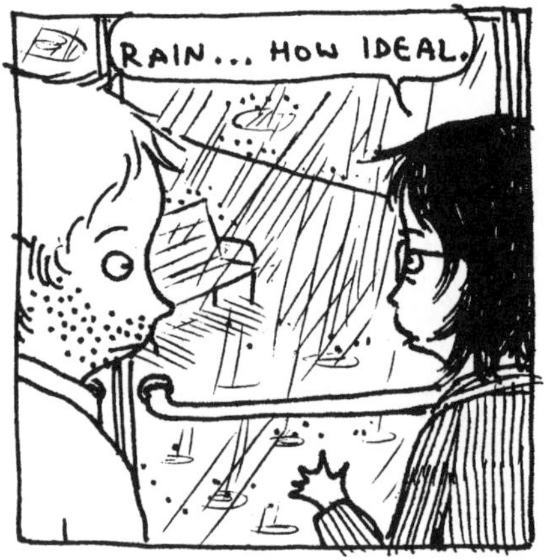
RAIN... HOW IDEAL.

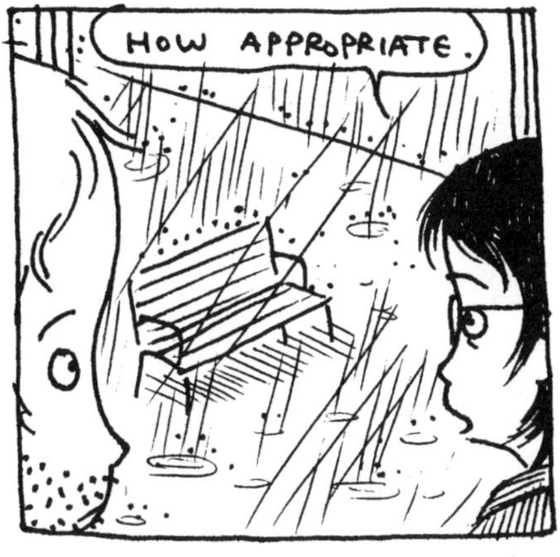
HOW APPROPRIATE.

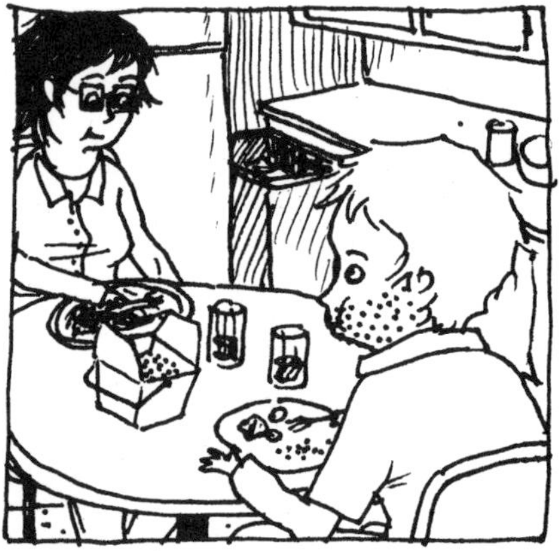

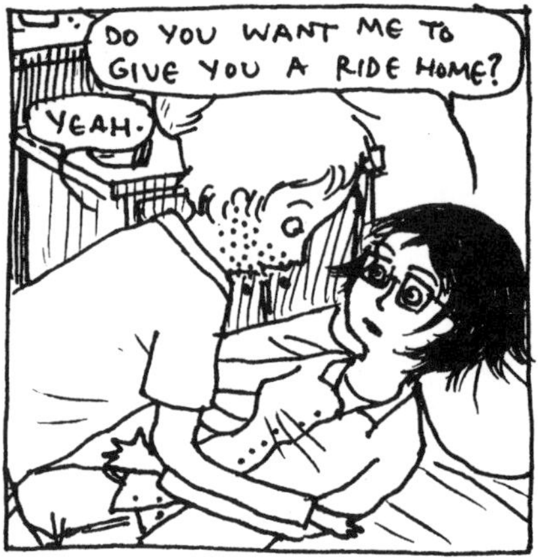
DO YOU WANT ME TO GIVE YOU A RIDE HOME?
YEAH.

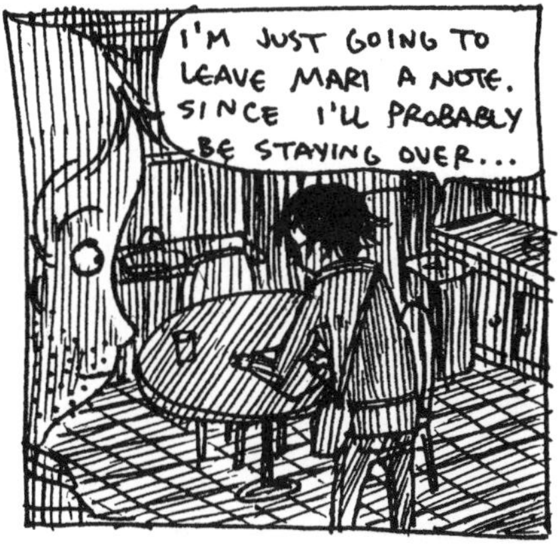
I'M JUST GOING TO LEAVE MARI A NOTE. SINCE I'LL PROBABLY BE STAYING OVER...

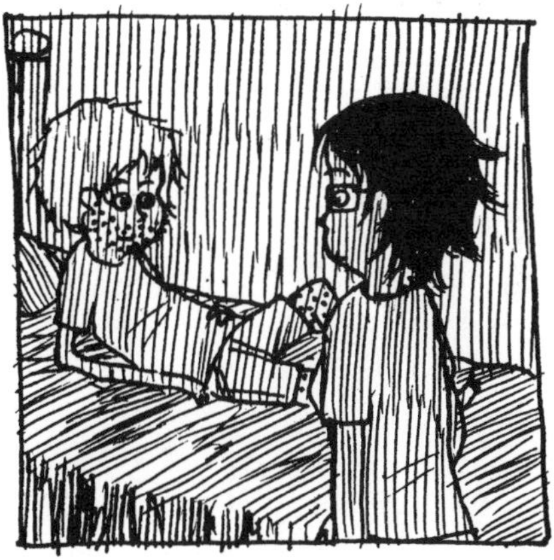

SOMETHING ELSE

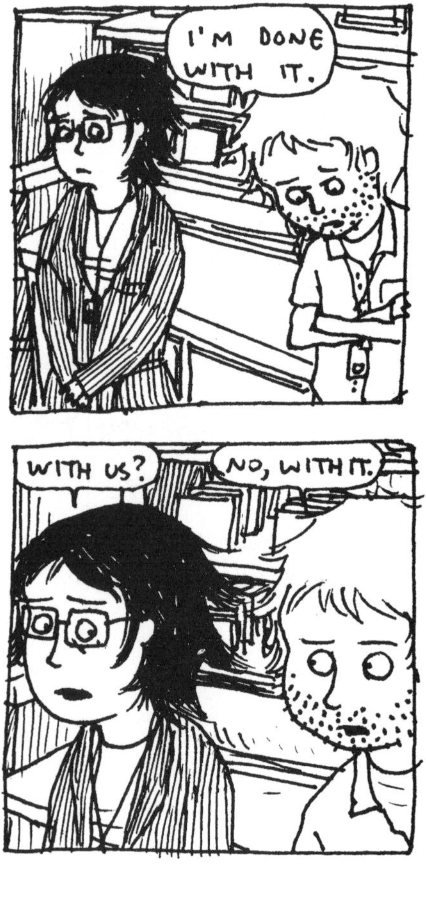
I'M DONE WITH IT.
WITH US?
NO, WITH IT.

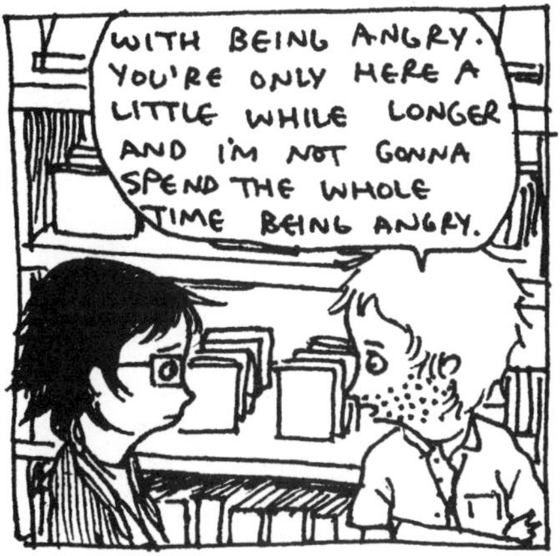
WITH BEING ANGRY. YOU'RE ONLY HERE A LITTLE WHILE LONGER AND I'M NOT GONNA SPEND THE WHOLE TIME BEING ANGRY.
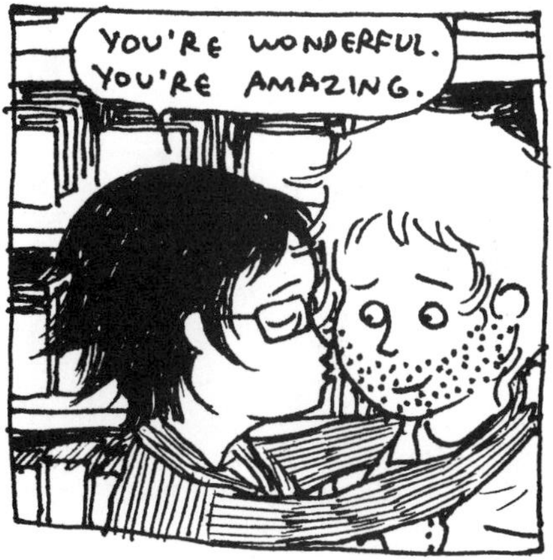
YOU'RE WONDERFUL. YOU'RE AMAZING.

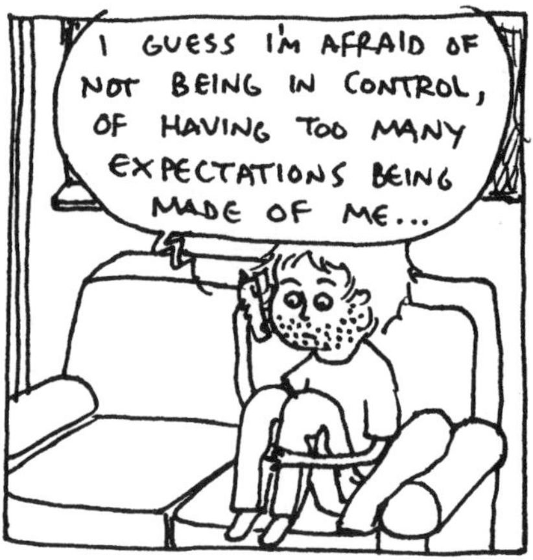
I GUESS I'M AFRAID OF NOT BEING IN CONTROL, OF HAVING TOO MANY EXPECTATIONS BEING MADE OF ME...

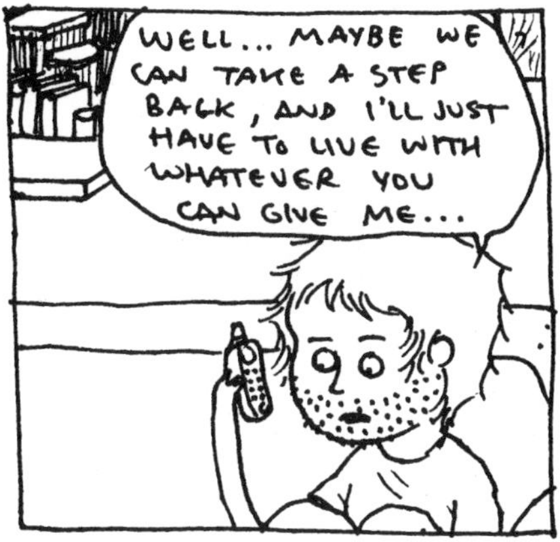
WELL... MAYBE WE CAN TAKE A STEP BACK, AND I'LL JUST HAVE TO LIVE WITH WHATEVER YOU CAN GIVE ME...

NOTHING SAYS I LOVE YOU LIKE

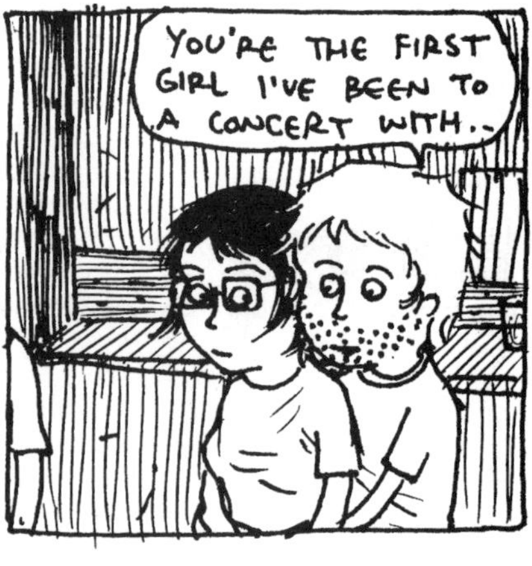
YOU'RE THE FIRST GIRL I'VE BEEN TO A CONCERT WITH..

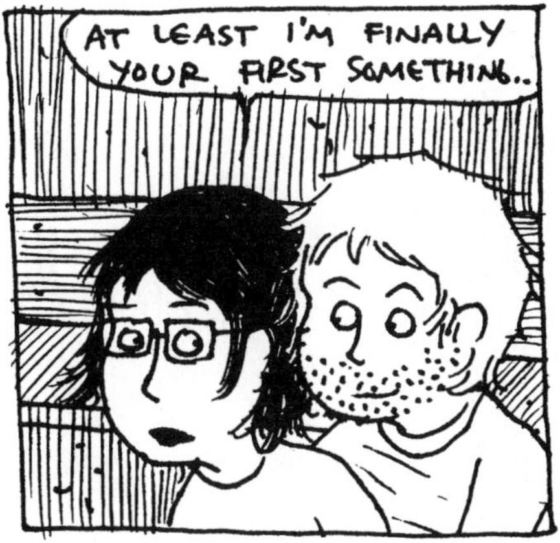
AT LEAST I'M FINALLY YOUR FIRST SOMETHING..

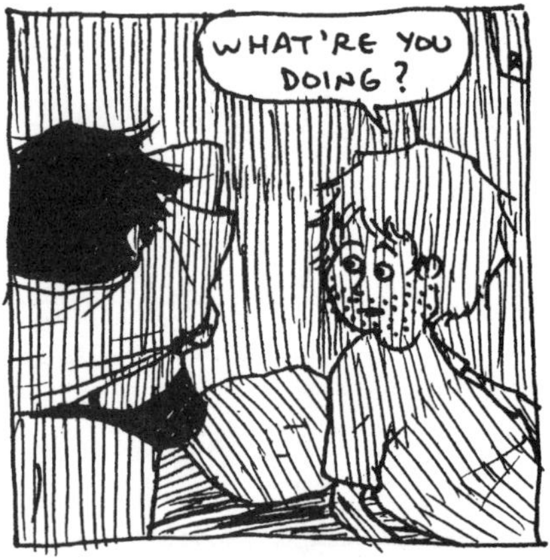
WHAT'RE YOU DOING?

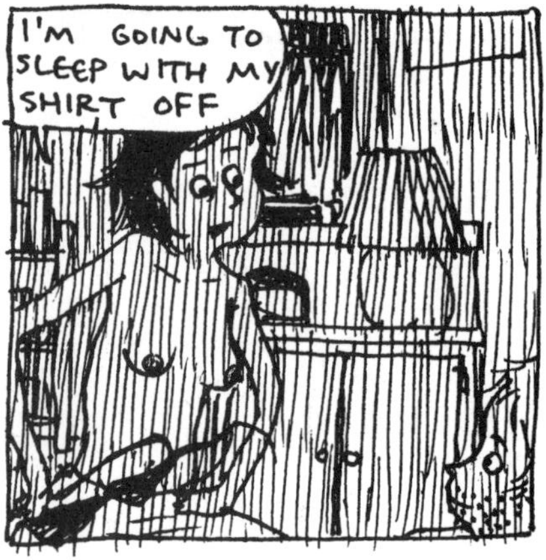
I'M GOING TO SLEEP WITH MY SHIRT OFF

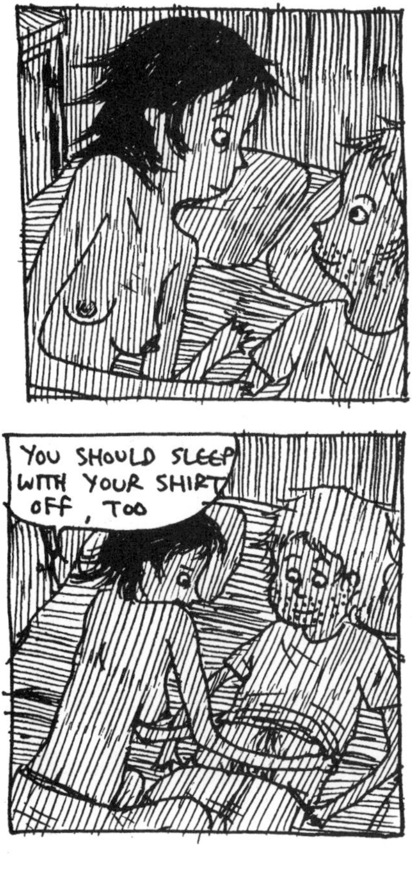
YOU SHOULD SLEEP WITH YOUR SHIRT OFF, TOO

...AND WE COULD LIVE IN A COZY LITTLE APARTMENT WITH A CAT...
...AND I'D COME HOME FROM TEACHING AND YOU'D ALREADY BE HOME 'CAUSE YOU WOULD JUST DRAW ALL DAY...

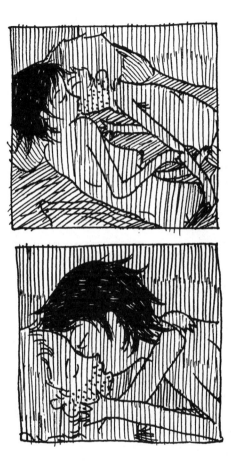

G R A D U A T I O N

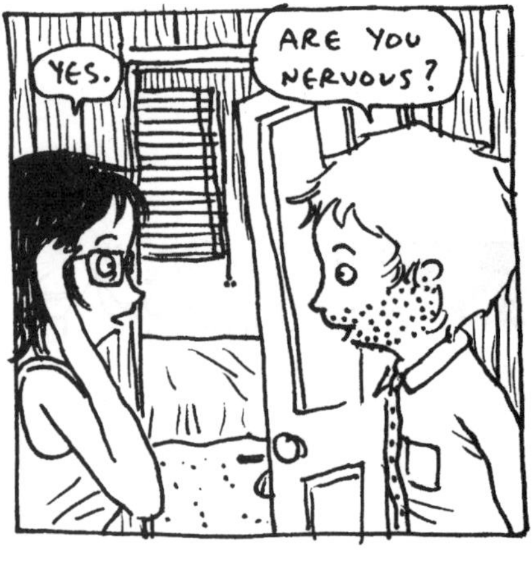
ARE YOU NERVOUS?
YES.

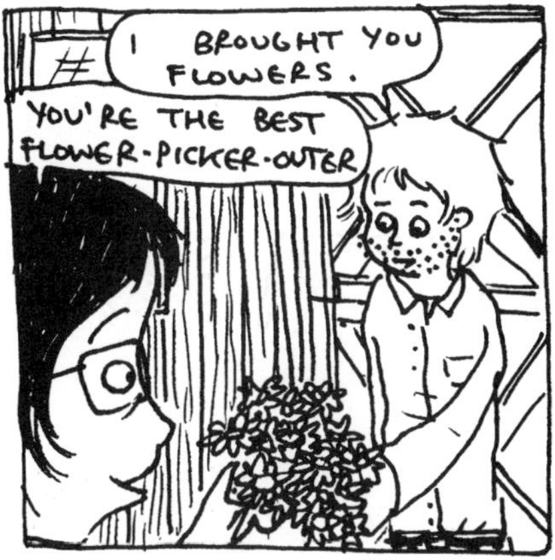
I BROUGHT YOU FLOWERS.
YOU'RE THE BEST FLOWER-PICKER-OUTER

MAY

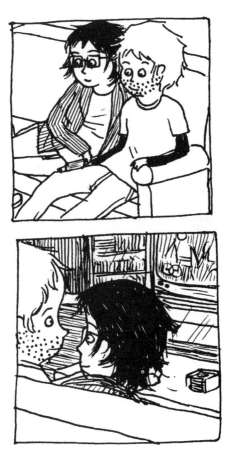

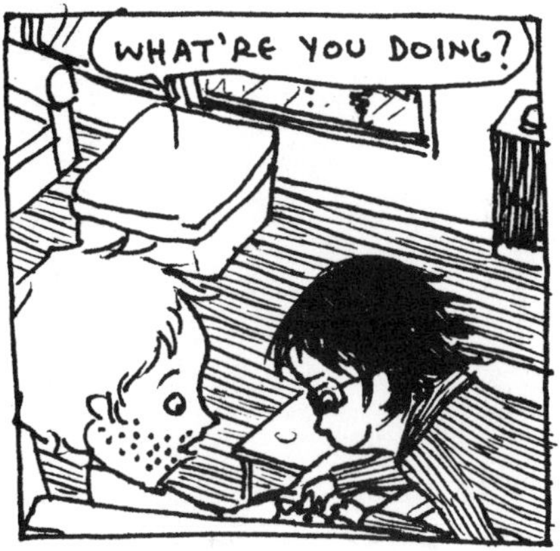
WHAT'RE YOU DOING?

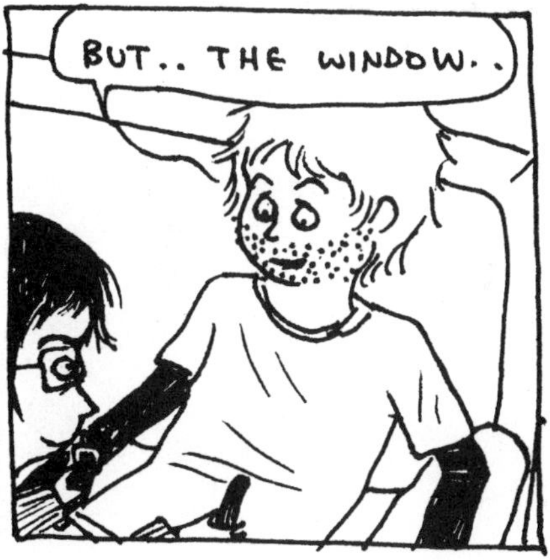
BUT.. THE WINDOW..

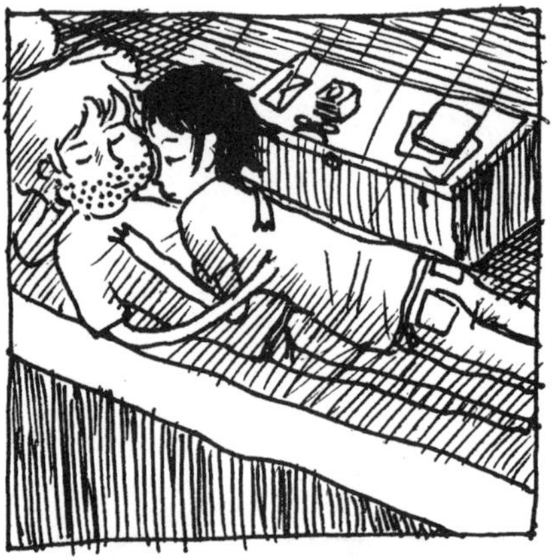

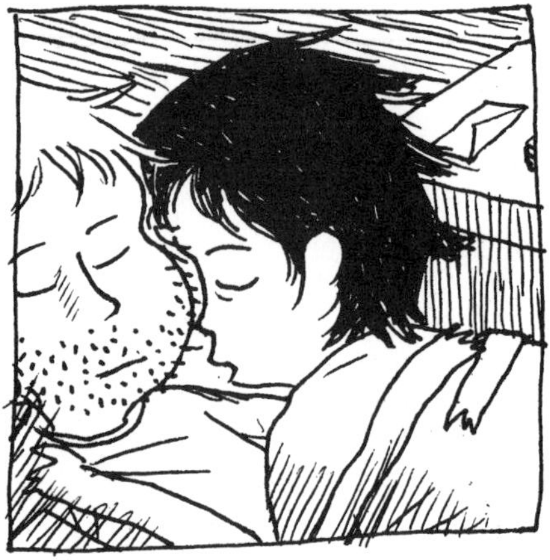

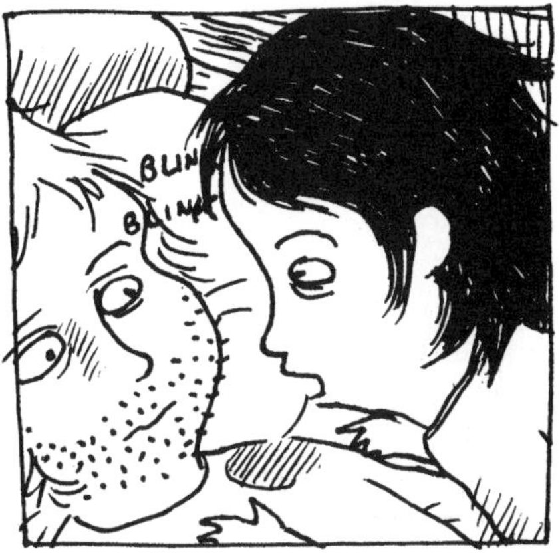
BLIN

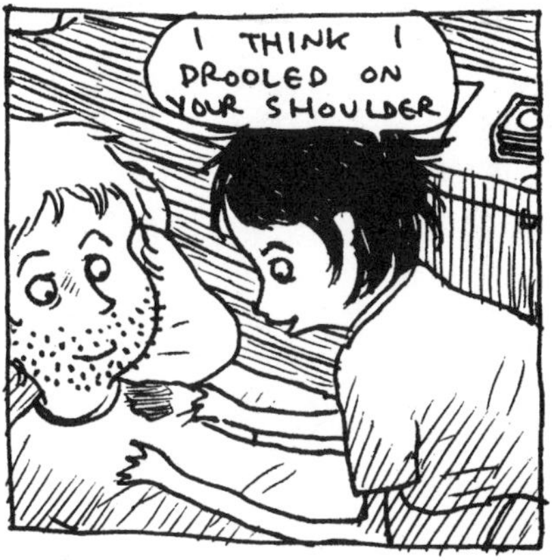
I THINK I DROOLED ON YOUR SHOULDER

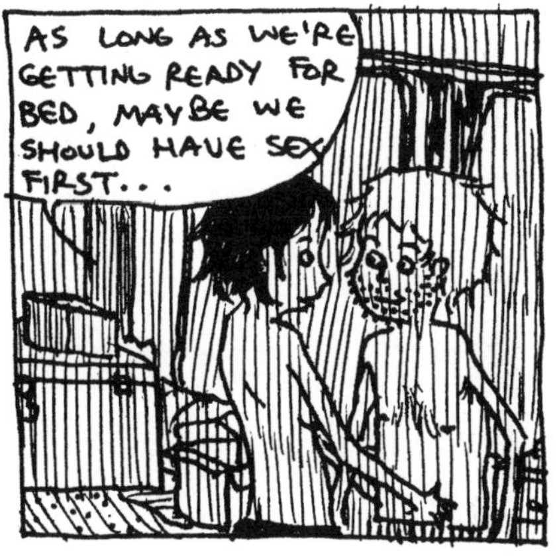
AS LONG AS WE'RE GETTING READY FOR BED, MAYBE WE SHOULD HAVE SEX FIRST...

M F A

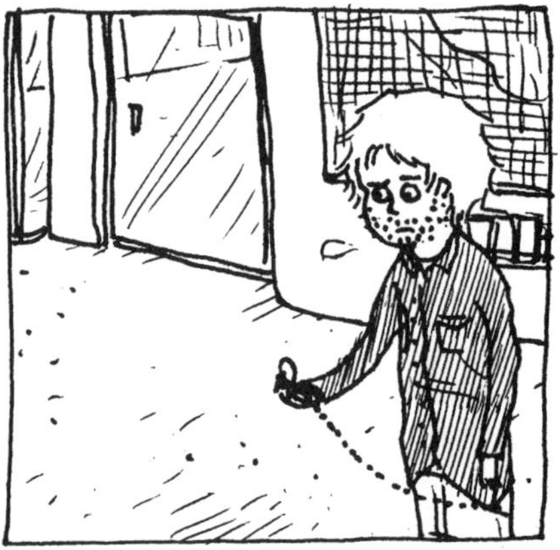

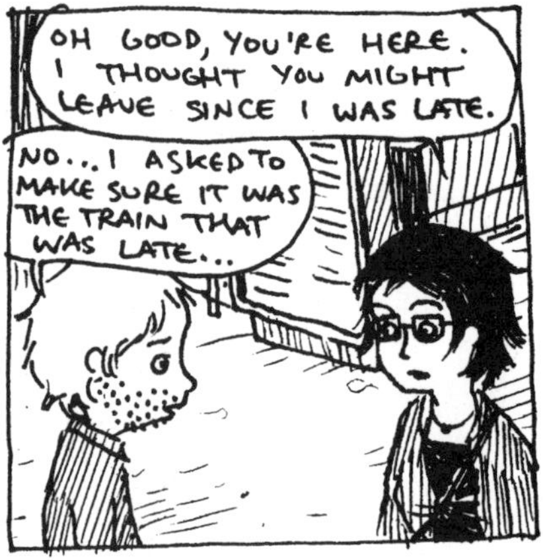
OH GOOD, YOU'RE HERE. I THOUGHT YOU MIGHT LEAVE SINCE I WAS LATE.
NO... I ASKED TO MAKE SURE IT WAS THE TRAIN THAT WAS LATE...

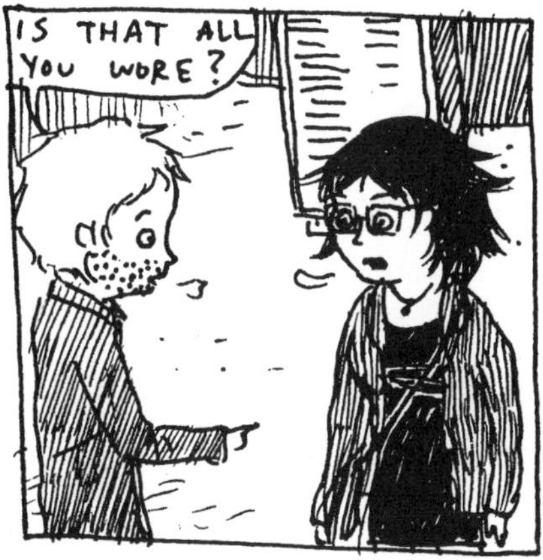
IS THAT ALL YOU WORE?

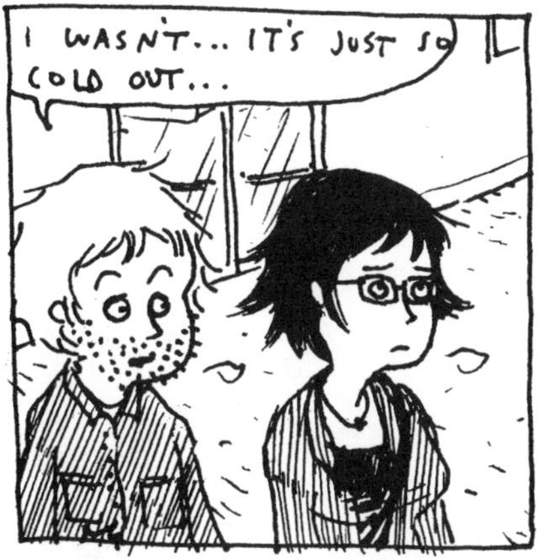
I WASN'T... IT'S JUST SO COLD OUT...

JUNE

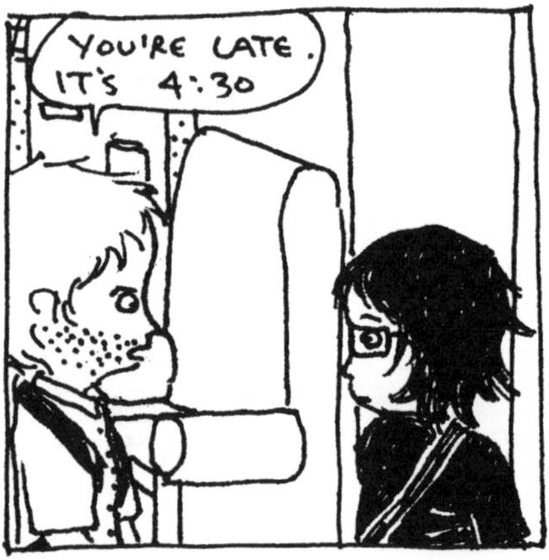
YOU'RE LATE. IT'S 4:30

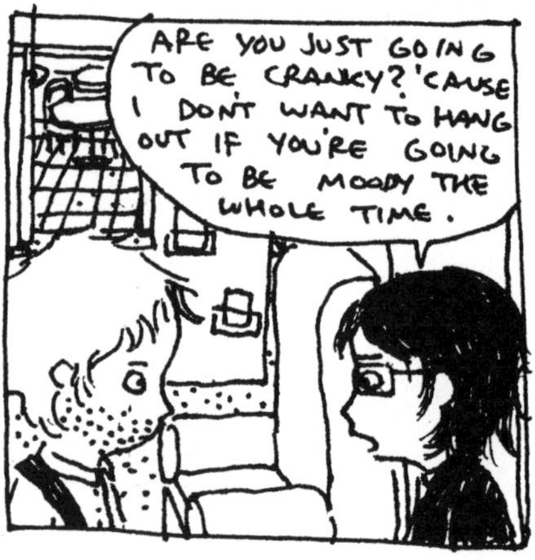
ARE YOU JUST GOING TO BE CRANKY? 'CAUSE I DON'T WANT TO HANG OUT IF YOU'RE GOING TO BE MOODY THE WHOLE TIME.

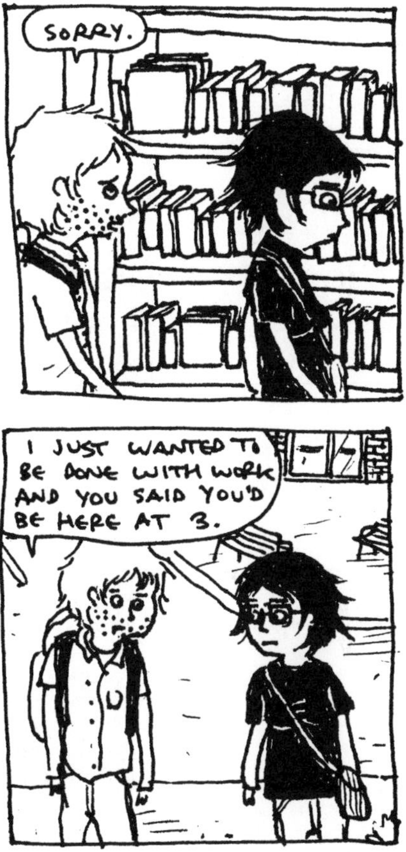
SORRY.
I JUST WANTED TO BE DONE WITH WORK AND YOU SAID YOU'D BE HERE AT 3.

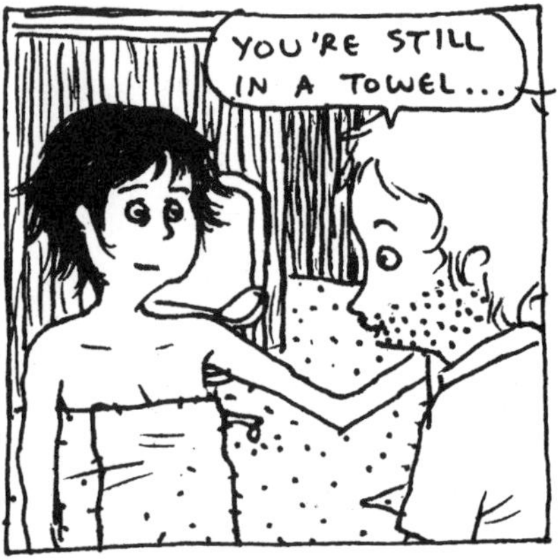
YOU'RE STILL IN A TOWEL...

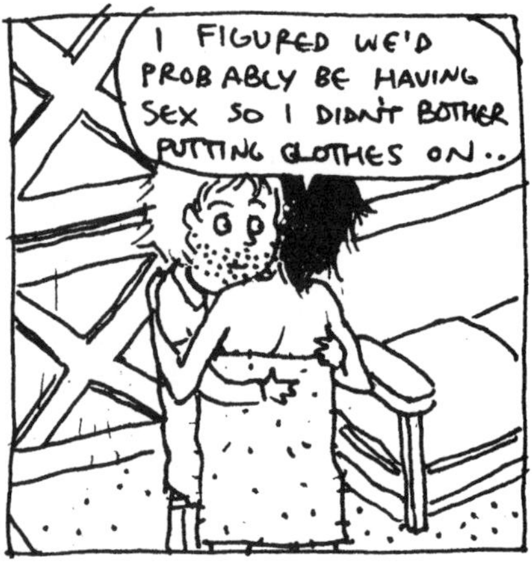
I FIGURED WE'D PROBABLY BE HAVING SEX SO I DIDN'T BOTHER PUTTING CLOTHES ON..

YOU REALISE IF WE GO TO THIS WEDDING I'M GOING TO WANT TO HAVE SEX WITH YOU AFTERWARDS

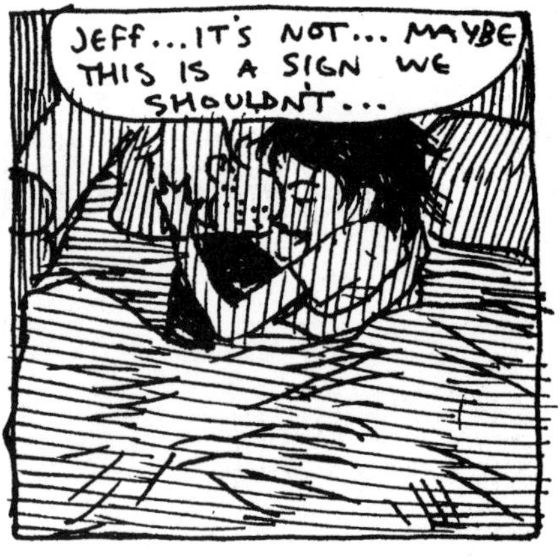
JEFF... IT'S NOT... MAYBE THIS IS A SIGN WE SHOULDN'T...

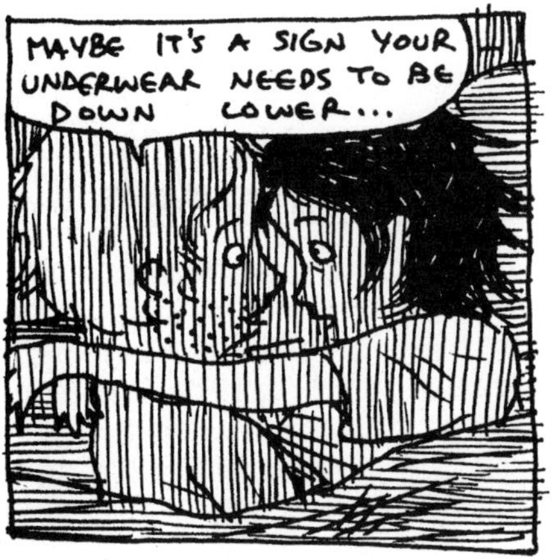
MAYBE IT'S A SIGN YOUR UNDERWEAR NEEDS TO BE DOWN LOWER...

LINGERING

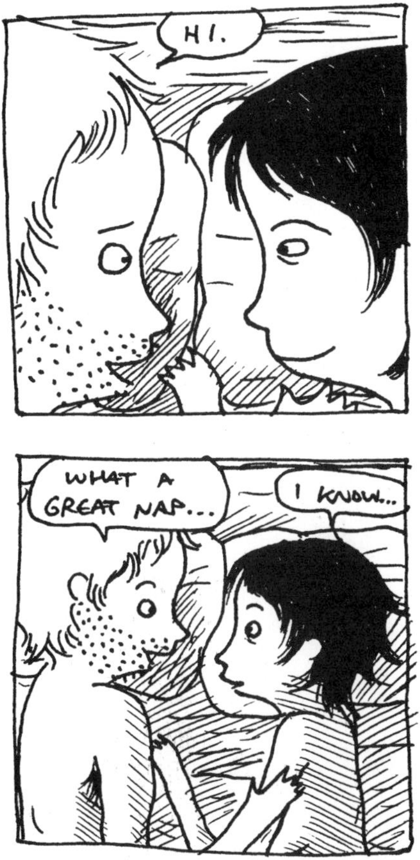
HI.
WHAT A GREAT NAP...
I KNOW...

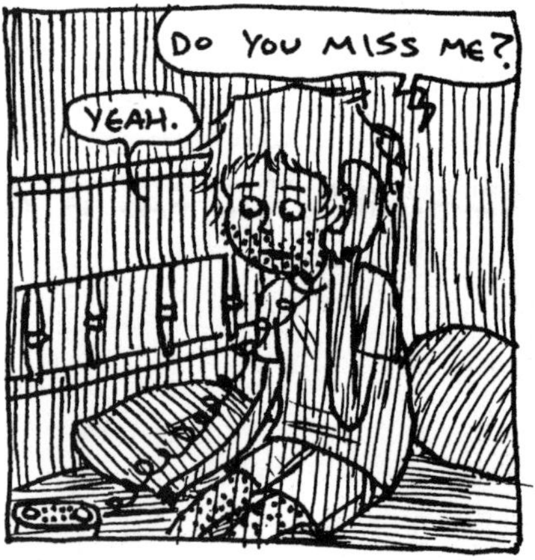
DO YOU MISS ME?
YEAH.

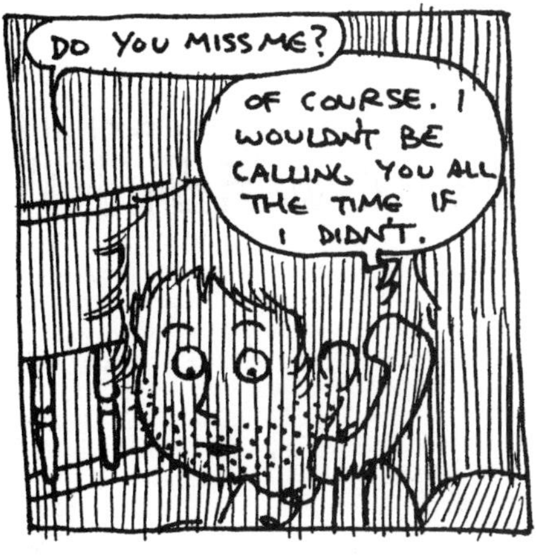
DO YOU MISS ME?
OF COURSE. I WOULDN'T BE CALLING YOU ALL THE TIME IF I DIDN'T.

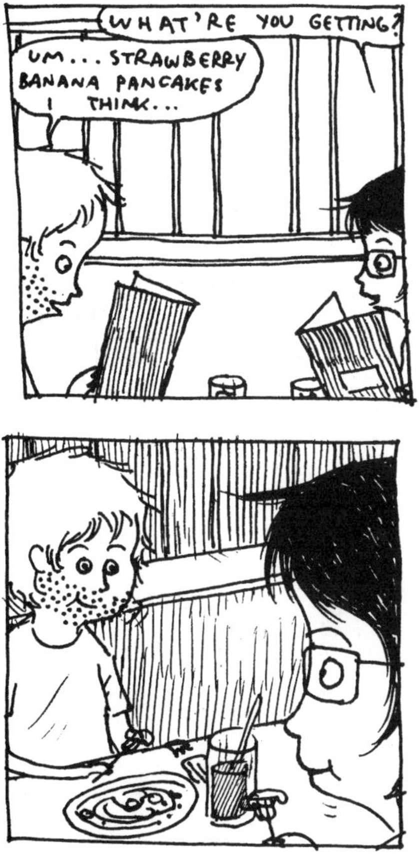
WHAT'RE YOU GETTING?
UM... STRAWBERRY BANANA PANCAKES I THINK...

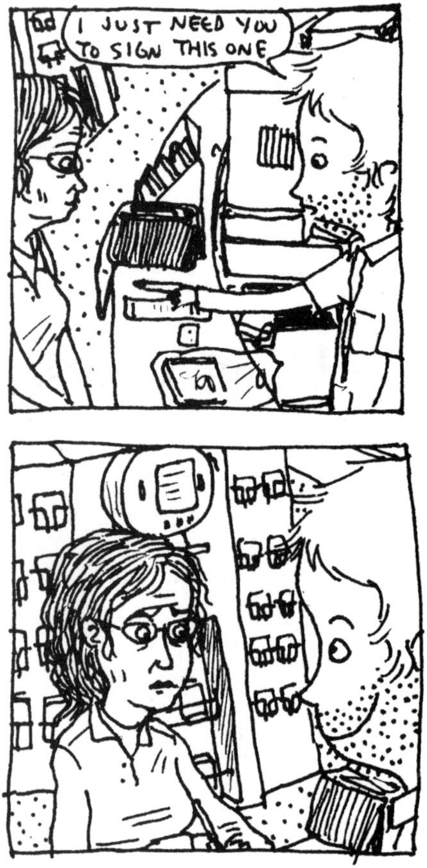
I JUST NEED YOU TO SIGN THIS ONE

YOU LEFT SOMETHING HERE.
WHAT?
YOUR UNDERWEAR.
OH... HEE HEE

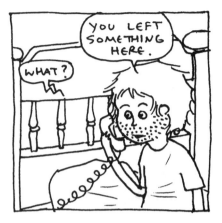

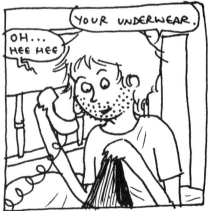

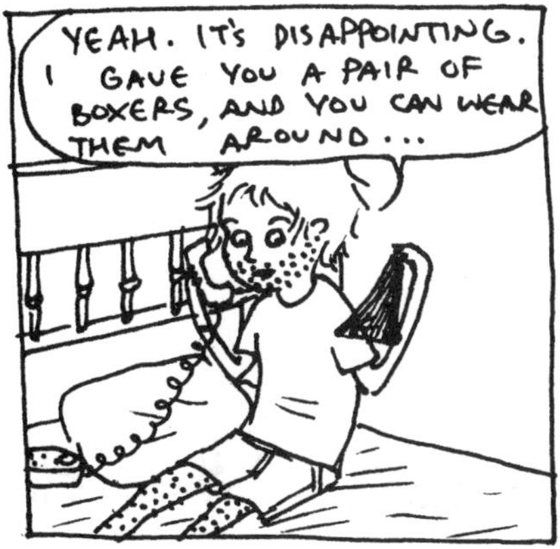
YEAH. IT'S DISAPPOINTING. I GAVE YOU A PAIR OF BOXERS, AND YOU CAN WEAR THEM AROUND...

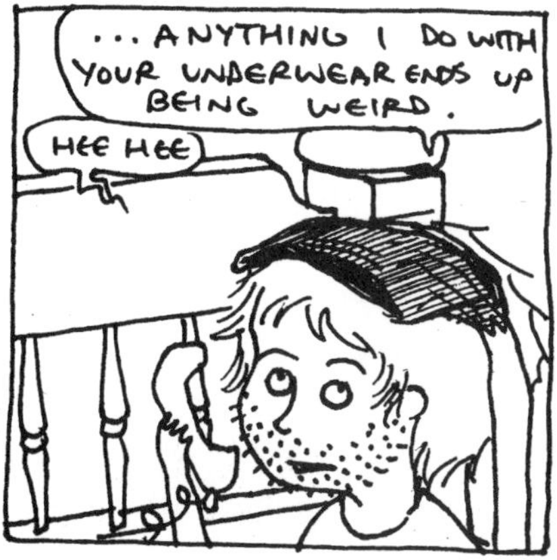
...ANYTHING I DO WITH YOUR UNDERWEAR ENDS UP BEING WEIRD.
HEE HEE

JULY

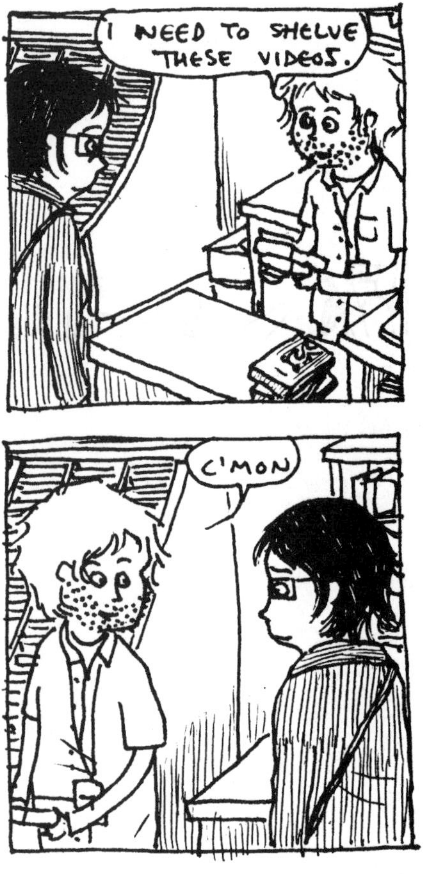
I NEED TO SHELVE THESE VIDEOS.
C'MON

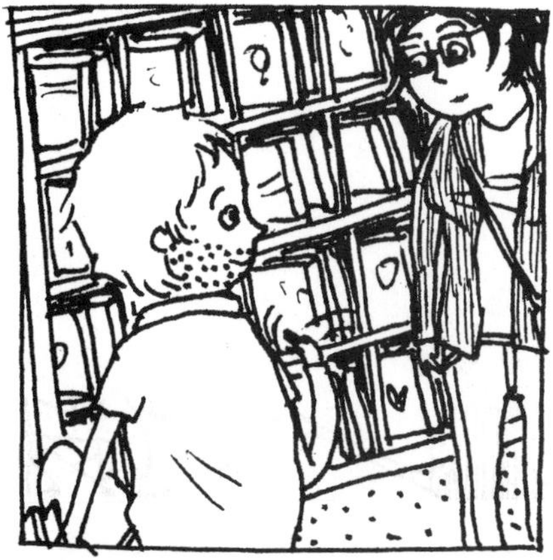

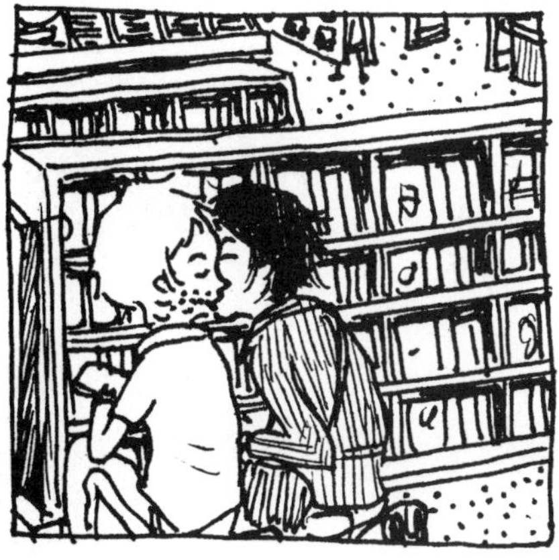

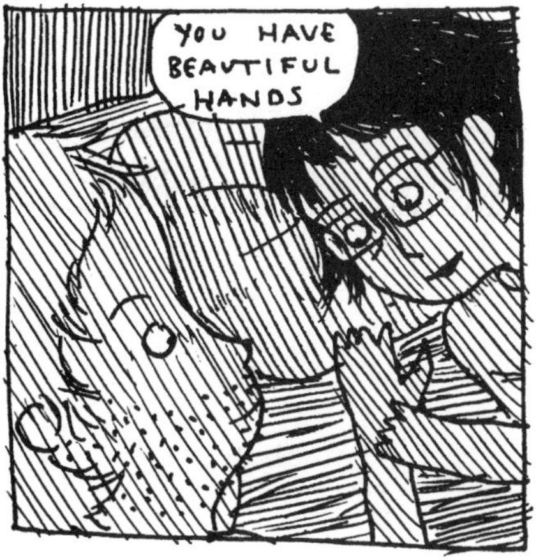
YOU HAVE BEAUTIFUL HANDS

VISIT

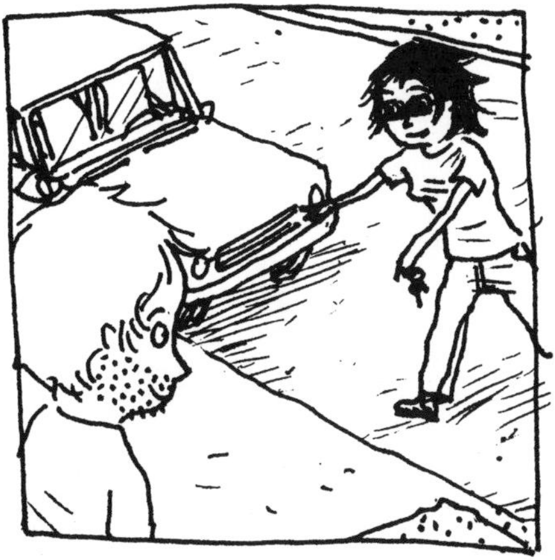

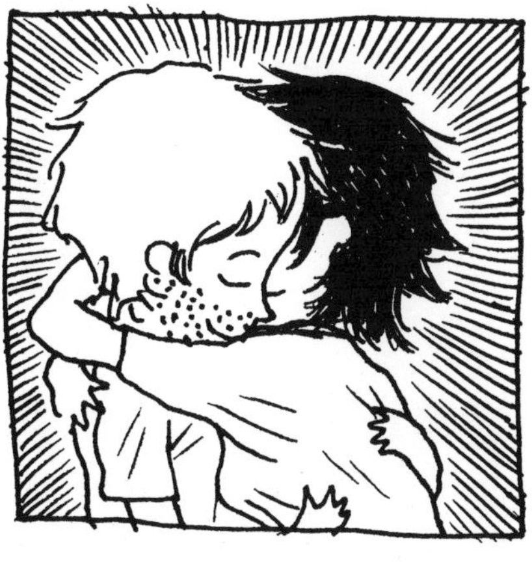

SOUNDTRACK

SIDE 'A'

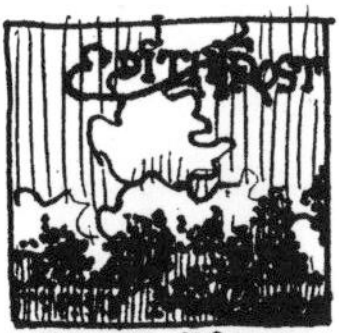

EDITH FROST
"WONDER WONDER"

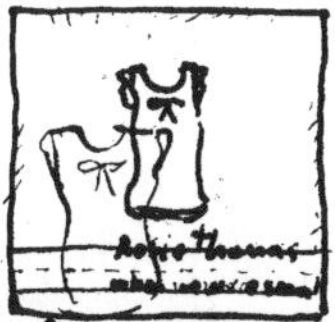

ROSIE THOMAS
"WHEN WE WERE SMALL"

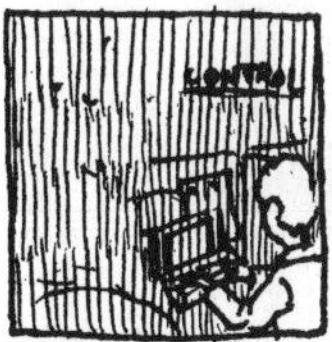

PEDRO THE LION
"CONTROL"

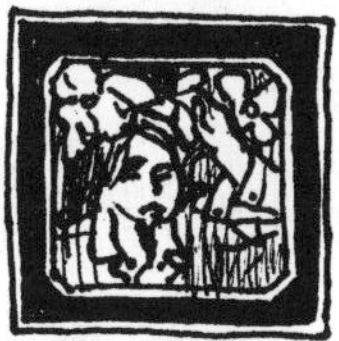

CAT POWER
"MOON PIX"

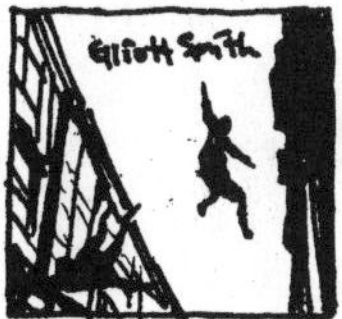
Elliott Smith

ELLIOTT SMITH
"ELLIOTT SMITH"

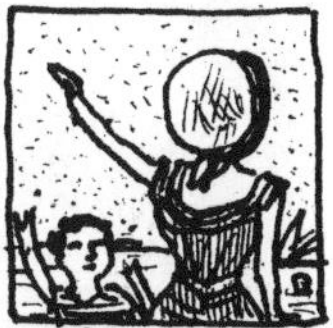

NEUTRAL MILK HOTEL
"IN THE AEROPLANE OVER THE SEA"

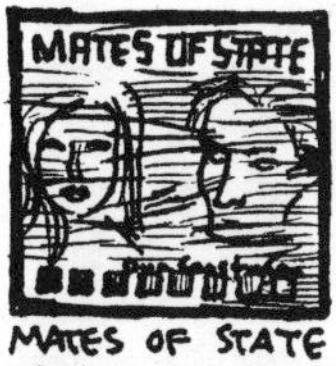
MATES OF STATE

MATES OF STATE
"OUR CONSTANT CONCERN"

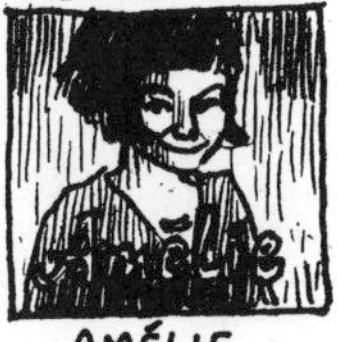

AMÉLIE
SOUNDTRACK

SOUNDTRACK
SIDE 'B'

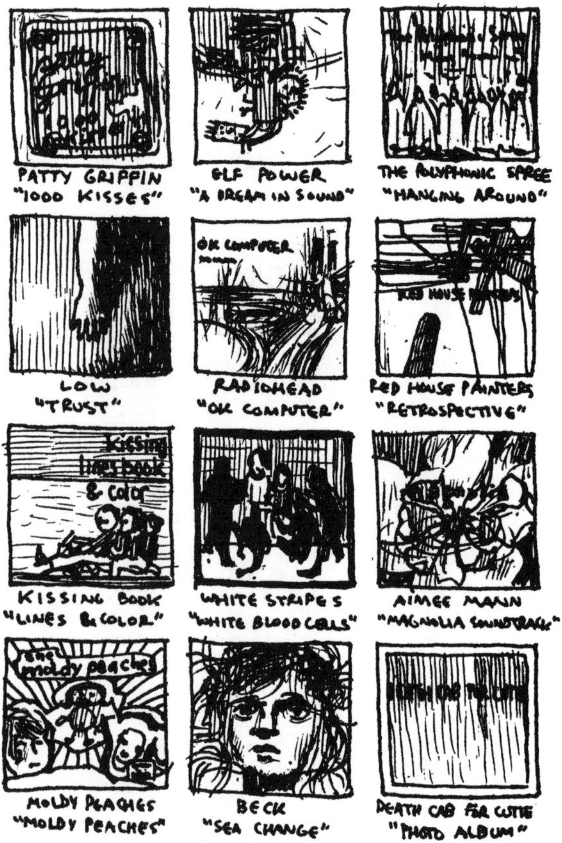

PATTY GRIFFIN
"1000 KISSES"
ELF POWER
"A DREAM IN SOUND"
THE POLYPHONIC SPREE
"HANGING AROUND"
LOW
"TRUST"
OK COMPUTER
RADIOHEAD
"OK COMPUTER"
RED HOUSE PAINTERS
"RETROSPECTIVE"
Kissing
lines book
& color
KISSING BOOK
"LINES & COLOR"
WHITE STRIPES
"WHITE BLOOD CELLS"
AIMEE MANN
"MAGNOLIA SOUNDTRACK"
the
moldy peaches
MOLDY PEACHES
"MOLDY PEACHES"
BECK
"SEA CHANGE"
DEATH CAB FOR CUTIE
"PHOTO ALBUM"

ALTHOUGH BASED ON ACTUAL
EVENTS, THIS BOOK LEAVES SO
MUCH LEFT UNSAID THAT YOU
MAY AS WELL CONSIDER IT TO
BE FICTION. TIME AND MEMORY
HAVE A WAY OF DISTORTING
THINGS, AND SOPHIA'S SIDE
OF THE STORY IS NECESSARILY
LACKING. PERHAPS SOMEDAY
I WILL BE RECONCILED WITH
HER BUT UNTIL THEN THIS
BOOK IS DEDICATED TO SOPHIA,
WITH APOLOGIES, REGRETS,
THANKS, ANGER, SADNESS, LOVE
AND A MILLION OTHER MIXED
EMOTIONS.

JEFFREY BROWN CURRENTLY
LIVES IN CHICAGO. YOU CAN
WRITE TO HIM AT:
jeffreybrownrq@hotmail.com
OR
P.O.BOX 120 Deerfield IL 60015 USA

SEE MORE AT:
www.theholyconsumption.com

RELATED WORKS

UNLIKELY
256 PP $15

How I Lost
My Virginity

CLUMSY
224 PP $10

A year long
long distance
love affair

AVAILABLE FROM
www.topshelfcomix.com